PENELOPE WILCOCK

# Spiritual Care of Dying and Bereaved People

MOREHOUSE PUBLISHING
HARRISBURG, PENNSYLVANIA

First published in Great Britain 1996
Society for Promoting Christian Knowledge
First published in the U.S.A. 1997 by

**Morehouse Publishing**

*Editorial Office*
871 Ethan Allen Hwy.
Ridgefield, CT 06877

*Corporate Office*
P.O. Box 1321
Harrisburg, PA 17105

A catalog record of this book is available from the
Library of Congress

ISBN 0-8192-1672-0

# Contents

*For Martin Baddeley*
*who taught me always to ask*
*the question*
*'What kind of God?'*

*and for Godfrey Johns*
*whose friendship I have treasured*

# *Foreword*

Penelope Wilcock is a British minister whose very thorough experience appears to be as Chaplain mainly to institutional, perhaps urban, hospices, which tend to be the norm in much of Britain and in some US cities. Nevertheless, hospice always being hospice in all settings, I found the book invaluable to, and highly reflective of, my own experience as Chaplain to an upstate New York bi-county and mainly very rural hospice. Here, most team care is given in people's often remote houses and farmsteads.

Ms. Wilcock's book is theologically and humanistically sound, in my view. It is incarnational as to its Christianity and deeply human as to its spirituality, the author being both ecumenical and inter-faith, as well as versed in ministry to those professing no particular faith. No narrow dogma on the one hand; no pseudo-mystical uplift on the other.

The style is clear, graceful, and authoritative; it is also subtle, yet as wide-ranging as penetrating. Ms. Wilcock does not indulge in "poetic" prose, yet she uses imagery with grace and economy. Examples: "windsurfing on silence" as a way of establishing communication without speech; "holding the bowl [of life] under the waterfall of the holy." (The latter image took me straight back to the hot summer porch of an old battered farmer whom I baptized there, one nurse reading a lesson, another holding a silver bowl, and the man saying, as the water sluiced through his hair and down his cheeks, "Oh God, but that felt good!")

Here is one of several perfect aphorisms: "Jesus is not in the eye of the beholder, but in the kindness of God." Here, as often in Wilcock's writing, I was reminded of Frederick Buechner at *his* best. And, a rendition of something all of us in hospice, or any who have worked with the dying, have felt: "When a person dies, an extraordinary thing happens, in the spiritual dimension: it is as though a puff of energy—like the ink trail of a squid, the wake of a ship, the smoke, dust and flame of a rocket launch—is released into the lives of those who had a special connection with the deceased person."

What Ms. Wilcock does in this short-but-packed book is to move us, chapter by chapter, through every phase of the care she is so steeped in. First, she establishes that dying and grief are *spiritual events* which happen "on holy ground." Next, we move through how caregivers to the dying establish that peaceful, pain-free, safe environment which allows hospice sojourners to "*live* into their deaths." Then she speaks of how we are present to the dying by means of silence and listening as well as speech; and by touch and other non-invasive intimacies, such as sharing tears and laughter, the trivial and profound, and by sacrament and symbol.

After the "anticipatory grieving" of the dying and the family and the after death grieving of those left behind, we explore with Wilcock the ins and outs of funerals, memorials, and other commemorations; and, in a chapter devoted to the dreads and opportunities-for-ministry in this area, "AIDS, Fear and Love." She concludes with (again) timely observations on euthanasia and suicide (physician-assisted or not) in a final chapter called "Deciding to Die."

Throughout her book, Ms. Wilcock always promotes life, but is never didactic, judgmental, nor intolerant of other views.

While I have said that everything in her book chimes with my own and our team's experiences, Ms. Wilcock also *illuminates* those for me, or helps me see new things in them. At the same time, I was fed insights I'd never thought of—for just one example, to the Christian on the verge of death, of the nighttime setting of the Last Supper/Lord's Supper, and of the words, "In the night in which he was betrayed..." in view of "betrayals" by our bodies or minds, and in view of that one night, with its Supper Table and its Garden, being the eve of *Jesus's* life.

*Spiritual Care of Dying and Bereaved People* is an important book, and all the more timely as one is aware of the US Supreme Court's January 1997 hearing on physician-assisted suicide; and as one notices how many newspaper columns discuss the latter, or euthanasia, without ever mentioning hospice care as an obvious, and to me preferable, alternative to either.


*(The Rev.) Sheldon Flory*
*Episcopal priest and Pastoral Care Coordinator*
*Ontario-Yates Hospice (retired)*

# Holy Ground

## HOLY GROUND – BIRTH AND DEATH

The subject matter of this book is life, not death. Spending time with the patients in the hospice where I work, I have often been struck by the atmosphere of expectancy. When the people who are with us approach death, there is a sense of awe, the solemnity of a great moment approaching. A sacred moment.

I have sensed that atmosphere before, once; in the antenatal ward of a maternity hospital, where again there was a certain electric tension of waiting, a sense of souls looking all one way towards a great approaching moment. Birth, and death: charged with the holy, with mystery, entwined with pain, with the loss of self and the looking up to something beyond self. Birth and death, moments where onlookers may lose their nerve and run away, shaken by the terror and the cost and the power of the holy. For birth and death, being intense moments flaming with life, are holy ground.

Time and again, patients reflecting on their feelings when anticipating admission to the hospice say that they had looked on the prospect with dread. They had thought of it as a kind of 'Valley of the shadow of death', a place that should have 'Abandon hope all ye who enter here' nailed over the door. And arriving, they had been relieved and amazed to find it a place of light, airy and full of flowers; a place of laughter and creativity; a place where people dress nicely and eat well – a glass of wine and a manicure as much as a syringe driver and a catheter. As they relax in this warm, life-loving atmosphere, it is also a relief to find a place where the expression of fear and grief and anger is acceptable, and understood. The hospice offers a safe place to suffer, and a place of peace to die, because it is a place where people really live, sometimes for the first time.

For in confronting the business of dying, which all of us

have to face on many levels, we are not talking about turning our backs on life, we are daring to be led into the very heart of living.

How we face up to dying – our own dying, other people's dying, the agony of bereavement – will tell us much about ourselves. The sacred territory of death is a place which asks questions of us. Is it hard for me to be honest? Is it frightening to find myself in a situation of physical, spiritual and emotional intimacy with someone? How do I feel about deep helplessness – the moments when I can do nothing, say nothing, only be with you? Or would I rather walk away from that? When you confront me with your confusion, and your grief, can I look at that steadily? Or do I take refuge in evasions and lies?

As I look at those questions as part of learning how to accompany people on the spiritual journey of their dying, I realize that these are not issues of a different category from life; these are the questions I must face if I want to make dying a time when I truly live. If I never face these questions, then I will never have lived, no matter how young and healthy my body may be.

Spiritual care of the dying is not the special province of the clergy; it is not the thing we call in the expert for. It is the dimension of care for the dying which energizes and brings meaning to the days of journeying to the eventual farewell. It is the responsibility and privilege of each one of us to allow ourselves to become a touching place, giving space and permission to people to find a truth which dignifies and heals. It is for any of us, by the quality of our touch, our gaze, our presence, to communicate the heart of God – 'I am with you.'

To accompany other people, along with their loved ones, up to the gate of death, is to enter holy ground; to stand in an awesome place where the wind of the Spirit blows, to encounter peace and grief, insight, intimacy and pain on a level not found in ordinary living.

'Take off your shoes,' God said to Moses. 'You are on holy ground.'

Shoes desensitize, and they protect. They are needed for the practicality of our daily journeying. But we take them off on holy ground. Our feet are the site of many nerve endings, susceptible to pain. We protect them. Not on holy ground.

This is the place to lay aside that which desensitizes, and that which protects. If there is any way to offer spiritual care to bereaved and dying people without oneself becoming emotionally wounded, I do not know it. Medical professionals find ways to evade involvement, to retain detachment: but what medical care can hold at arm's length, spiritual care must embrace. And it is costly.

> Take off your shoes, for you are on holy ground.
> Become vulnerable, for you are on holy ground.
> Be sensitive, for you are on holy ground.
> Lay down your defences. You are on holy ground.

So here, right at the outset, the Christian minister (this word will be used throughout to mean spiritual carer, and can refer to either a lay person or a clergy person) runs up against the problem of Almighty God. I suspect that other religions have their variants on this problem too, but I write from the viewpoint I am at, which is the Christian religion.

Whatever else a god is, it is the personification of our ideal, that which we aspire to. We cast our gods in the image of ourselves, and we don't know ourselves. Thus our unconscious aspirations and ambitions gain a frightening hold over us when we harness them in the name of religion. We piece together a mosaic of ideals received in childhood or adopted since, and we project them forth as a being, and we say, 'This is God.' Then, what kind of god we have understood God to be determines our ethical and moral constructs, our outlook on life.

The commonest concept of God that religious tradition has fostered is 'Almighty God'. The God who can do anything. The God who initiates rather than responds. The God, therefore, whose favour is understood in terms of things going well for me. The God, as the Bible says, who heals all your diseases, who prospers you and blesses you with well-being, fertility and comfort. Thus the absence of well-being, health, prosperity, or whatever, can be felt by people who have been brought up on such a concept of God as a signal that God is angry with them, or that they have somehow become cut off from God's power and love, or that God was never really there at all. For people who have been brought up on the traditional concept of 'Almighty God', the spiritual reappraisal involved in

3

the journey towards death is often characterized at the beginning by disappointment, anger, bewilderment, disillusionment and fear.

The Communion Service of the Church of England opens with the prayer:

> Almighty God,
> to whom all hearts are open,
> all desires known,
> and from whom no secrets are hidden . . .

'Almighty God' is one of the key determining concepts of the Christian Church. 'For the kingdom, the power, and the glory are yours', we pray.

This can seriously inhibit us when we face the journey of dying, because as worshippers of 'Almighty God', we run into trouble when we experience helplessness. Helplessness is not that which we aspire to, it is that from which we flee. Helplessness is the opposite of almightiness. Helplessness has no place in the image of God we have developed. Therefore our counsel often instinctively combats helplessness: 'Don't cry'; 'Be brave'; 'Be strong.' Likewise our response to the helplessness of others is to take rescuing action, to be the cavalry coming over the hill (and it follows that our response to our own helplessness is shame).

It requires little reflection to perceive that this approach breaks down in the spiritual care of dying people and their loved ones.

Firstly, because we can no longer act to save them. What is inevitable for all of us has arrived for them. They face their mortality, and we are helpless to prevent this.

Secondly, because it is *they*, not we, who are the protagonists in this last act of life. The work of dying is theirs, not ours. Ours is to travel alongside, as companions on their journey.

Thirdly, because this act is an act not of power, but of weakness. It is the work not of building up, but of laying down, of achieving not mastery, but acceptance.

I once met a Jesuit priest, an intelligent and scholarly man, well educated in both psychology and theology, who told me that he could never do the work I do, journeying alongside people who are dying, because he, in such work, would feel so helpless. I set him at his ease with the reassurance that this is not everyone's calling (though in another sense, of course, one day it is), but I made it clear to him that spiritual care of dying people is not undertaken by a marvellous strain of humanity who confront pain and grief and suffering with calm confidence. We all feel helpless accompanying the dying; and there is a good reason for it too: it is because we *are* helpless. Medicine can help with pain, nausea and other physical distress, but there is no bypassing or anaesthetizing the grief of the laying down of life.

Painfully, those who do not run away learn that our own helplessness is a gift to those who are helpless; that our consenting to live at peace with our own mortality and inadequacy permits them also to be at peace. Our acceptance of helplessness in ourselves and in others disarms the shame learned in the shadow of 'Almighty God'. By the side of the dying we learn stillness, waiting, simple being; the arts of quietness and keeping watch, prayer beyond words.

It is not an easy lesson. I recall a young woman, who died of a motor-neurone disease, in the last weeks of her life. She was moved out of the main ward into a side room, and thereafter her consultant never came to her bed. Medically, he had no more to offer. The simple act of entering the room where her mother kept watch at her bedside, to enter for thirty seconds that arena of helplessness, either did not occur to him or seemed too costly. And he was not the only one. Despite her medication, she had phases of acute pain, and I remember her mother's distress one morning, saying, 'She cried all night, in pain, crying. All night. And no one came in at all. They must have heard her. She cried all night, *all night*, and no one came.'

Once we have learned that our helplessness is a gift to the helpless, we can stay with them in peace; but it is not an easy lesson to learn. Too often, medical professionals shy away from the presence of the dying, not because they are callous, but because they cannot bear their own helplessness, because they live in the shadow of 'Almighty God'. The spiritual care of that dying woman was given by her mother, who, with tears rolling down her face, tenderly stroked her daughter's hair through the sweating, wrenching pain, saying quietly, 'I'm here with you, sweetheart. Mummy's here.'

This is not to say that our sense of our own helplessness should inhibit us from actively caring for dying people. Those responsible for spiritual care should join their vigilance to that of all the team of carers around a dying person to ensure that action is taken to guarantee that their physical care is of a high standard and their environment is appropriate for their needs. The addressing of our own helplessness is necessary to stop us running away, or taking refuge in false optimism, or withholding from the dying person permission to explore with us their fears and grief.

If it is true, as I believe it is, that the kind of God we have understood God to be determines our ethical and moral constructs, our outlook on life, then clearly we have to review our image of God to undertake the spiritual care of dying people. 'Almighty God' will not do. To undertake this review requires a reopening of the Gospels and the Old Testament to recover the vision of a God who weeps, who hurts, who suffers his heart to break.

We need to look again at the God of the Old Testament who shakes his fist in helpless – yes, helpless – anger at his beloved people who abandon him, who are indifferent to his needs – yes, *needs* – and then relents because he loves them, helplessly. There is no love without helplessness, no love without need, no love that does not yearn for an answering love. Helplessness, yearning, need; these belong inescapably to the nature of love: and God is love.

We look also at the Gospels, for Christianity is a revealed religion; we believe in the revelation of the nature of God in Jesus Christ, the ultimate Word, the out-breathing of God. And there in the Gospels, God is found first as a baby, dependent on others to carry him, feed him, clean him, keep him warm, teach him to speak, come to him, talk to him, cuddle him. Almighty God?

The baby grows up into Christ the healer, teacher, miracle-worker. Yes, but also Jesus the homeless man, the one who was dependent on others for a bed to sleep in, a roof over his head, a meal in his belly. Jesus with a price on his head, with a traitor among his closest friends, and a family who thought he was mad. Jesus whom they said was possessed by devils, whom they tried to stone, whom they plotted to hand over for execution. A revelation of God that includes struggle, uncertainty, risk.

Then the Gospels recount the story of the Passion. Jesus sobbing in Gethsemane, broken in the pain of abandonment, terrified at the prospect of crucifixion. Jesus humiliated and scourged, stretched in anguish on the cross. Jesus laid in the ultimate abandonment to the providence of God, as a corpse, in a borrowed tomb.

It is in the context of that helplessness that the Christian faith locates its most daring doctrines: salvation and resurrection. Truly those doctrines assert the power and sovereignty of God, but focused in this man we call Emmanuel, the Word of God, the revelation of the divine nature. 'Almighty God'?

The tradition of the Church has tagged on the words 'the kingdom, the power, and the glory are yours' to the prayer of the man Jesus, which otherwise expresses a simple abandonment to God's provision and grace. To accompany the dying on their journey, we need to peel back the tradition of 'Almighty God', and find the curious, paradoxical reality of strength-in-weakness which is the outworking of grace. On this holy ground, we cease pumping theological iron, to find the vulnerability of God revealed in Jesus.

Before we come to face our own death and the death of those we love, before we make that awesome, holy journey, and in order to care wisely for those who make it now, we need a less narrow image of God. We will both live and die better if we understand the sacred necessity of abandonment to the gospel of grace.

Perhaps from time to time we might alter that opening prayer of the Communion Service to 'Vulnerable God, to whom all hearts are open, all desires known, and from whom no secrets are hidden . . .'

Our secrets are not hidden from God. The things we are afraid of, and cannot bring ourselves to disclose. The things we are ashamed of, that reduce us to whispering, our heads bent, our faces hidden. The things that hurt, that we cover up, dreading the tears that would flow if we forced such hidden secrets into the open. From our vulnerable God, no secrets are hidden. To the God who suffered helplessness in Jesus, with all that meant, our hearts are open. To the God who

yearns and longs and aches and reaches out, our desires are
known.

Maybe, sometimes, we should begin our Communion
Service with simpler words:

> Vulnerable God,
> You understand.

## IDENTITY AND PERSONHOOD (see also Ch. 5)

Spirituality is all about who one is, and that is found only in
relationship with other people, with our own inner reality, and
with God, whatever we conceive God to be. Therefore one
of the first tasks of a spiritual carer is to affirm the patient's
personhood and identity. It is essential that the minister or carer
has some idea of what it is to be a person, because there is by
no means universal agreement as to the nature of personality.

In the Hebrew scriptures, God is sometimes called YHWH,
and the consonants are derived from the verb 'to be', so that
this name of God could be translated 'I am that I am' or 'I
will be what I will be.' This lack of exact definition suggests
an ontological flux and fluidity, which is also present in humanity – made in the image of God. We call ourselves human
beings, but we could also maybe think of ourselves as human
becomings, a 'will be' as much as an 'is'.

Personhood can be looked at with the help of various
different models, some much more static and inflexible than
others.

Some people see personhood as very static, and for this
understanding of personhood we might take the model of the
stone. A stone is a substance of unchanging nature, the same
tomorrow as today. It can be modulated (e.g., made into sand
by the action of other stones and the movement of the sea) by
long processes, but its selfhood is essentially established and
consistent. I remember meeting a close friend for the first time
after some months and saying to him, 'I feel shy with you, as
if you were a stranger. I don't know who you are now.' He
looked at me and replied, 'I'm just the same as I ever was. I
haven't changed.' His view of personhood is the stone one. He
expects to be in October what he was in July, unless something
unforeseen and unlikely occurs.

# Holy Ground

## The Stone

Ephemeral _____ x ___Permanent

Other people understand the concept of being as less fixed, but still fairly consistent, and for them we might use the model of the building. A building is basically unchanging, but accommodates different functions (as a house may be sometimes a family home, or the venue of a political meeting or a party), according to which its self-definition may vary. The building can be added to by extension, partly demolished, renovated, repaired or altered, sometimes radically, but on the spectrum of possibilities between ephemeral being and permanency, it is towards the permanency end of the spectrum.

Women often think of themselves in the terms of this model: 'I am John's wife. I am Sue and Kevin's mother. I am a school secretary. I am a local preacher. I wear so many different hats, and which is the real me?' A sense of personhood being essentially static but accommodating a variety of functions.

Women are also more likely than men to think of their body image in terms of this model of personhood. Extended by pregnancy, renovated by cosmetic surgery, partly demolished by hysterectomy or mastectomy, redecorated daily with moisturizers and make-up, extended and demolished by growing fatter and dieting: but still retaining an essential, unchanging self. A person with this concept of self, especially near to death, may want help to explore and discover the core self, if there is a feeling of having lost the sense of that original self somewhere among the changes and rôles that have been experienced.

## The Building

Ephemeral _____ x _____Permanent

But it may be that personality is not after all so static. For some people, personality can be understood according to the model of the flame, a constantly changing, subtle form of energy. This form of being is not easily encapsulated or pinned down, its nature lying more in its warmth and light and movement than in the more concrete, reliable forms of the stone and the building.

# The Spiritual Care of Dying and Bereaved People

This understanding of being also incorporates the sense, which the other two do not, of interdependence. A flame cannot live alone, it must be fed, or it dies. Sometimes in the swimming pool I have looked at the dancing, shimmering pattern of light reflecting from the surface of the water against the wall, and this is another picture of this understanding of personality; changing, shimmering, constantly modulating, created out of environment and nourishment. Artists and actors are more likely than most to identify with this model – those who are only truly alive when they are writing or engrossed in a sculpture, those for whom drama or dance or conversation or preaching is the mode through which they become. These people find themselves in relationship and in vocation, and in times of chronic illness and, to a lesser extent, when approaching death, they may suffer a sense of loss of self, of uselessness, unless the right environment can be provided for them to burn again in relationship and the exchange of ideas.

### The Flame

Ephemeral _____ x _____ Permanent

A final model is that of the colour. Some people see themselves as coming into being with others, created by a combination of circumstances and other personalities. Today is rainy and I have dreary chores to do, and I feel blue. But you come along, my mellow yellow friend, and together we merge into a peaceful green. Or today is a cheerful day, today I am yellow. I may encounter someone I just can't find a way to relate well with, our colours don't blend, and beside them my yellow looks muddy, or insipid. Or I may meet a friend with whom somehow I always end up laughing, a warm rosy friend, and together we are orange, witty and warm. Touched by the pink of a gentle, comforting friend we may become peach. Depending on the dynamic, the possibilities range from rainbows to mud!

In illness or adversity such a person may need support to find the colour of courage and hope and humour, rather than becoming the personification of withdrawal and despair. Looking at this model of personhood, it becomes clear that the way you are with me is a gift of selfhood to me: I am (or become) a person who is ashamed or ignored, a person who feels loved or beautiful, an empowered person, affirmed and worthwhile, a wretched embarrassed person, according to what I see in your eyes, the colour you reflect back to me.

The Colour

Ephemeral ___ x _____ Permanent

This sense of self as a constantly modulating, newly discovered, intangible mode of being is the one I have myself – hence my conversation with my 'stone' friend, my uncertainty about who he was now, who we would be together. Every day and every relationship is like an artist's palette, loaded with possibility. This is why *loving* is the mission of the God who is creator and redeemer. For loving is that which ultimately is most likely to create loveliness, and to redeem a self from a becoming of cynicism and destruction to one of wholeness.

## THE UNITY OF PERSONALITY

In addition to retaining the flexibility to understand personhood along a variety of lines, it is important to understand something about the unity of personality. The Christian religion is very helpful here, because it has already started us off on this mode of thinking with its doctrines of the Trinity; God (in whose image we are made) as multiple while being essentially one. In the same way, a person who is whole and healthy in his or her inner being is integrated – one. However, this oneness is not simple, but is the integration of a whole repertoire of modes of personality, which under stress and fear and illness can break down into conflicting splinterings and fragments, selflets living in a confused and threatening world where nothing makes the sense it did and the inner harmony of integrated personality is lost. And yet, despite and beyond this, there is a further, deeper unity, as it were a 'flavour', the unique aroma or taste of *that* particular person, which, even though it may only be glimpsed, returns, survives, cannot be lost. One of the tasks of spiritual care of those suffering confusion and dementia is to try to reach through the muddle to touch the essential being.

Further to this, each person will have developed a chosen image or 'front', and depending on how authentic this image is in expressing the reality of the person, this 'front' may have become very brittle and insecure in serious illness. Much gentleness will be needed to help a person lay aside an image which is a defence, a hide, needing dismantling if real peace of spirit is to be enjoyed.

There is an old-fashioned phrase 'making a good death', which for devout Christians used to require the confession of sins and absolution by the priest; the shriving of the soul. But this task of dying well can be expressed as making one's peace with God or of finding one's own inner peace, depending on the spiritual frame through which the dying person views the world.

For Christians, the teaching about human being is that God is entwined with us at our very roots. This is expressed in the Genesis story of the creation of Adam, who was moulded of the stuff of earth, until God breathed into him and he became a living being. The Hebrew word for breath can also be translated as spirit or wind, so the creation story explains the mystery that that which makes God divine – Holy Spirit – is the same as that which makes humanity human. God breathed into Adam God's spirit, God's breath, God's essential self – and Adam became a human being, came to life.

Therefore, from the Christian point of view, to find one's true self and to find God is the same journey. That is why Jesus spoke of healing as salvation, saying not, 'Be cured of your disease,' but 'Go in peace, your faith has saved you/made you whole.'

For this reason, 'making a good death' and integrating healthily the experience of bereavement both start with the exploration of the question, 'Who am I?' – to myself, to my carers, to those I love. And spiritual care begins with finding and affirming the human being or human becoming, and saying 'yes' to that reality.

There is a story told of Jesus at the dinner party of a man called 'Simon the leper', who is a Pharisee. A woman 'with a bad reputation' (a prostitute, tradition surmises) gatecrashes the party and begins to wash Jesus' feet with her tears and wipe them dry with her long loose hair (respectable ladies bound up their hair). The Pharisee watching with some disapproval thinks to himself that if Jesus were really a prophet he would *know* what kind of woman this person is and not permit her to make him ritually unclean by personal contact.

Jesus turns to the Pharisee and he says, 'Simon' (his *name*, not his shame, 'leper', or his religious rôle, 'Pharisee'), 'do you see this woman?' (Luke 7.44).

The task of spiritual care begins with that question of Jesus, 'Do you see this woman? Do you see this man? Neither the rôle nor the reputation, but the person?' The beginning of spiritual care of dying and bereaved people is in learning to see.

FLEXIBILITY – THE NEED TO MOVE WITH THE SITUATION

The model of personality as flame or colour (pp. 10–11) requires a flexible approach, as the needs of the individual will be varying and responsive, dependent on the chemistry of relationship. In this understanding of personality, one minister may be better than another for any one patient – unlike the Building model, where any good plumber or bricklayer will do; or the stone, which can be modelled by any good sculptor. The more sensitive and *alive* is one's concept of personhood, the more the need for flexibility in approach and relationship will be apparent.

Further, as a person draws nearer death, physical changes impose a need for increasing flexibility: vomiting, incontinence, sleepiness, confusion, unconsciousness, all alter the requirements of spiritual encounter.

Not only are physical realities more pressing, but this tends to be a time of stripping away, when honesty and authenticity become urgent, when games, etiquette and social formalities can be distressingly irrelevant, draining, and a distraction from spiritual purpose. Having said this, religious *ritual* can be very meaningful, being useful as a means of expressing solemnity and seriousness of purpose. The sacraments and anointing come into their own here (these subjects are discussed later, in Ch. 4).

Since the acknowledgement and affirmation of identity is an essential foundation stone of spiritual care, it follows that flexibility to accommodate the differing requirements of individual personalities and circumstances will be a high priority in a nursing environment which takes spiritual care seriously.

I remember Bernadette, a devout Catholic, who prayed daily from her little black prayer book and loved to pray the rosary. When she came into the hospice and needed somebody to help her say her prayers as she grew weaker, the nurses encountered a problem with her prayer book. It was so old and well-used that it had long disintegrated, and the pages were in a higgledy-piggledy sequence that made it impossible for one unfamiliar with the prayers to follow. So the nurses asked me if I would come and say her prayers with her, which I did. Most often we used to pray a decade of the rosary together and then add a few extra prayers on the end. Bernadette grew weaker and eventually drifted into unconsciousness, but I still came every day to say at her bedside the prayers that she herself had prayed as long as she could. On one day, as I sat there, glancing down the ward to the next bed, I found myself both heartened and amused by the situation. Here was I, a Methodist, praying the rosary at the bedside of a Catholic no longer able to say the prayers herself, while at the next bed a nurse was very gently and carefully lifting to the lips of a woman no longer able to feed herself her favourite tipple of sherry. It is this tailor-made response to the needs and preferences of the individual that affirms identity and is reassuring of personal worth. It is this, and not religious talk or long counselling sessions, that is the beginning of spiritual care.

In order to ensure the flexibility of care that a spiritually caring environment must offer, it is probably vital, and certainly extremely helpful, that the caring team as a whole feel confident and unafraid about the spiritual dimension of their work, so that spiritual care is not seen as the province of a chaplain or clergy person alone.

Some nurses see the care they offer as limited to the physical and often strictly task-orientated. In talking about spiritual care with hospital and community nurses, time after time I receive the response, 'I never realized that *I* could offer spiritual care myself.'

Some doctors, especially hospital doctors, display extraordinary fear and a sense of inadequacy when access to their simple humanity rather than their medical expertise is needed. The training of junior doctors in hospital, with its emphasis on facts and knowledge (vital, of course!) rather than attitude, and its destructively exhausting timetable, seems to have a detrimental effect on doctors' ability to relate on the level of spiritual need. Doctors are often made too tired, too busy, too punchdrunk by their regime, to relate on a significant level with patients. It is remarkable they achieve the level of human relationship they do, but there is no doubt this could be improved by more time, space and better training in interpersonal skills. For patients often turn to doctors for counsel and comfort of the soul. This is natural, since patients perceive the doctor, who offers diagnosis and treatment, as one who understands their condition. And often patients think more holistically than medical professionals, conceiving of their condition in whole-being terms rather than disease classification. Therefore it comes naturally to feel that the doctor who 'understands how I am' will be able to respond with wisdom when I express how I feel. It can come as a shock of hurt, and feel like appalling insensitivity, if that doctor retreats behind a barrier of distance or formality, refusing eye contact or conversation or touch. The responsibility of spiritual care may not be one which doctors seek, but it is one which they will be offered, because of the trust, the authority and the power which come with the job.

In caring for dying people, there is a pressing need to move with the situation, to be open to the requirements of *now*. Many times I have been asked to have a talk with a patient who was indicating that anxieties, memories and griefs needed airing: but by the time I was available, the moment had gone. The moment of intimacy and trust arises within the context of a relationship, and should be dealt with as it arises. Very often it is those who perform the most basic and intimate tasks for a dying person – feeding, washing, helping with the commode or the catheter, holding the vomit-bowl – with whom the patient can feel the level of intimacy and nakedness of self to allow disclosure of deep fears and grief, of vulnerability kept hidden from those with whom relationships are less deeply intimate. Those who care for the basic bodily needs of patients, giving the relationship something of a parent–child quality, are those to whom tears and the hidden self will be entrusted. It is most important that the nurses who will be offered such trust are affirmed in their own sense of spiritual competence, to receive and honour the vulnerability and trust of another human being, not withdraw from it out of a sense of personal inadequacy, or try to put it on hold until the chaplain arrives.

Clearly it is also important that chaplains be prepared to roll their sleeves up and help with feeding, holding vomit-bowls, or whatever seems appropriate, for this will facilitate the intimacy of relationship that enables a sufficient level of trust for meaningful communication to take place.

In a hospice environment, where staffing levels are good and time spent listening to and being with patients is a priority, it is interesting to notice that not only do the patients benefit from the good quality of spiritual care and affirmation offered, but the morale among the staff is good too, and the resulting atmosphere of positive regard for human dignity and worth is experienced as healing, as peace.

Flexibility is essential also in considering the day-to-day needs of patients and their families. If a dying person needs to talk or to pray, it is helpful if possible to flow with that, rather than trying to make a later appointment to fit in with the minister's own schedule. The next day, speech or consciousness may have gone, or the patient may simply be too weary for conversation. In talking with bereaved people, it is often the case that conversation moves very swiftly in and out of the pain of grief and loss and the most banal, trivial chit-chat. Sometimes agony can be borne only in snatches, and sufficient time must be offered to enable the bereaved people both to look at and to look away from the loss they are trying to face.

A considerable amount of a chaplain's time is spent in simply hanging loose with patients and staff, talking and laughing over inconsequential things, and time spent like this is not wasted. It is thus that ground is established so that when a patient or family member or member of staff needs to talk, a friendship has been established, a foundation for trust. Also, as faculties diminish with illness, and maybe speech goes, the chaplain will know the idiosyncrasies and personal characteristics which enable this person to continue as a complete individual, living, not dying, to the very end.

# 2

# *Creating the Context*

## CLEARING THE ROAD

The book of Isaiah starts its fortieth chapter with a message of comfort. The '-fort' part of comfort has its roots in the same place as the word 'fortitude'. To comfort someone has both the modern meaning of easing their pain with gentleness, and its older meaning of imparting to them courage and strength. It also has the overtones that we associate with the word comfortable; something relaxing and familiar, something restful, cosy, homely and warm. A lovely word.

'Comfort, O comfort my people' is the opening prophecy of this fortieth chapter of Isaiah. The prophet speaks of a God who comes to people in pain and distress, people at the end of their tether. He says:

> In the wilderness prepare the way of the Lord,
> Make straight in the desert a highway for our God. (v.3)

The image is that of the arrival of a visiting king. The road along which he will come must be prepared for him. Stones must be removed and potholes filled; all obstacles taken out of the way to leave level ground for the king to pass along as he comes on his royal visit.

This is the task of good spiritual care, and it can only be achieved by a team working well together. Spiritual care is not an appendage to medical care. It does not inhabit a self-contained niche as the spiritual aspect of palliative care. Above all, spiritual care is not the urging upon dying or bereaved people of a philosophy not their own, however beneficial another view than the one they currently hold might seem to be.

Spiritual care for bereaved and dying people is the task of working in the wilderness, in the place where people are, the desert place of pain and loss, to remove the obstacles that obstruct the highway of the God who comes. Whatever form God takes in the mind of those who wait in the wilderness for a sign of hope, whether it be religious belief, or a sense of peace, a discovery that one is, after all, loved – *however* God is conceived of and received, the team will have done its job if the obstacles to that entry of spiritual equilibrium have been removed.

To comfort God's people (and that is *all* people, not just a select few) and make straight the road along which God may come to them, is the work of spiritual care.

It is teamwork, because the obstacles on the road are many, and need different disciplines to dislodge them. Pain; fear; physical discomfort (such as nausea); disabling and embarrassing symptoms like incontinence and involuntary movements; unfinished business in relationships; practical problems like the management of finance and environment; religious terror; inability to adjust to changing body image (e.g., after mastectomy); feelings of guilt or resentment; inability to sleep; loneliness: such as these block the road along which peace and wholeness, the *shalom* of God's presence, may come. Together, loved ones, doctors, surgeons, nurses, social workers, voluntary helpers and carers, chaplains, bereavement counsellors, physiotherapists, backed up by the help of people skilled in massage, reflexology, meditation techniques, nutrition, etc., can help to smooth the path along which peace may come.

It would be unrealistic to suggest that all such problems as I have listed can necessarily be solved or removed. Sometimes the problems can only be acknowledged: and that may be all that is needed. For example, a problem like loneliness can be a difficult thing for a palliative care team to address. Lonely people may lack friends and loved ones of their own, and have not been able to find in life enough reassurance to answer the existential ache of human being. A lonely person may have neither the skills nor the will to create a circle of loved friends; and the members of the palliative care team may not have the resources of time and emotional strength to offer any substitute for that missing network of relationships. But what the care team can offer is acknowledgement and recognition of the loneliness. When people know that their pain is seen, is heard, often the angriness, the inflammation, subsides from the wound, and healing can of itself begin.

Other, more tangible difficulties, such as the need for an

appropriate bed or a hoist, or the need for help sorting out changing financial requirements, can actually be solved and removed.

Good spiritual care is offered when the whole team works together in a holistic practice of care, so that the whole complex of distress is addressed, leaving the dying or bereaved person as free as possible to stand with dignity on the holy ground. Then, undistracted by the multiple nagging of anxieties, pains and regrets, the attention of the soul is available for the momentous spiritual experience of dying and bereavement.

Sometimes people do not want to look the God who comes in the face. Sometimes, even when the whole being is supported, comforted and loved, the realities of dying and loss are too much to look at. Distraction, conversation, the refuge of denial may be chosen instead, and the safe familiarity of daily trivia is a preferred option. And this is all right. The task of spiritual care is only to clear the road along which God may come, not to force anyone's feet along it. God offers, but does not demand, courage; stays with us, but does not compel us to look into his eyes.

In doing this, it is often the case that the work of the team will itself become part of the spiritual experience of the one on whose journey we are companions. I once had a conversation with a young man with AIDS. He was considering the way that, though he would never have chosen such debilitating illness and early death, AIDS had brought into his life many new relationships; people he had grown to love, people he thought were really wonderful. Good spiritual care had both combated his distress and added to his spiritual treasure.

This is a way of understanding the spiritual battle that St Paul writes of, when he says our struggle is not against flesh and blood, but against powers and principalities. When we bring comfort, we turn the tables, in some measure, on evil.

## SURROUNDINGS AND ATTITUDES

One of the resources of spiritual care is environment; physical, aesthetic, and also in terms of the ambience created by attitudes.

Openness and light are very important for people who are seriously ill and cannot remain in the familiar surroundings of their own home. If someone is coming into an unknown place connected already in the mind with death, then apprehension and fear will be hovering. A place which is dark and poky with many closed doors may reinforce fear. Open space and airy light introduce a different note, of optimism and relief.

Flowers, music, pictures, gentle (but not insipid) decor all help to reassure, as does the presence of the kind of furnishings that might be chosen for someone's home, not institutional or office furniture.

Smell is very important too. In a place where people have wounds that will not heal, digestive problems, incontinence and diseased body tissue, there can be many smells to combat. The smell of disinfectant fighting the smell of urine does not lift the spirits. Scrupulous attention to cleanliness is a primary necessity. The siting of the sluice in a well-ventilated place is important too. This may seem obvious, but I have worked in a place where the sluice was in a tiny room with no exterior walls (and therefore no window), opening off a central corridor (also with no window) enclosed by fire doors. The trapped stench from the accumulation of dirty incontinence pads filling the plastic disposal sack in there was stomach-turning, and its depressing odour seeped into the surrounding rooms.

Smell can be combated well by all the usual means of hygiene, air-fresheners, and by emptying commodes, disposing of dressings, etc., promptly. Also by more elegant additions; flowers, aromatherapeutic oils heated by nightlights (the burning flame also helps absorb smells). Wherever possible, eliminating the source of the smell is the priority action. Introducing pleasant fragrance is good for the soul; but powerful perfume disguising a bad odour is not a happy combination.

The smell of a place is among its most powerfully evocative characteristics, and will be strongly influential in shaping the mood of the people who live and work there. Our smell memory, almost indelible, is located in the deepest and most primitive part of the brain, and accordingly moves us at our deepest and most primitive level.

Perhaps more difficult to confront, but very important, is the sensitive question of the impact on the senses of *people*, as well as of the place. Spiritual carers are often well trained in their psychological techniques of approach, but not in the physical aspects of their task. If they are the employees or representatives of an institution (such as a hospice, a hospital, or the Church), they may have had expectations regarding dress outlined to them in terms of smartness, but not in terms of its appeal to the senses.

First impressions are very important. Professionals are used to looking smart and businesslike, but that is not required here. Visually, a spiritual carer should appear gentle and non-threatening, avoiding power-dressing and hard, boxy lines. Their clothing should be soft and matt in appearance: comforting and gentle rather than hard and shiny. Any jewellery should be light – humorous and idiosyncratic maybe, but not aggressive or violent. Colours should be considered in the same way: quiet or bright colours are good, but harsh clashes of colour (large black and white stripes with a bright green satin shirt or blouse, for example) may be smart and appropriate in the office, but do not work well to create the gentle, healing, accepting environment of spiritual care. It can also be unnerving for dying and bereaved people to discuss the subject of death with someone wearing unrelieved black.

The tactile quality of the clothes should be considered too. A spiritual carer may have to hold someone in their arms; and that may require a bit of stretching and leaning over if the patient is hard to reach because of therapeutic hardware equipment. So it helps if the carer wears clothes that will stretch and move: nothing too uncompromisingly tailored, nor a skirt so short and tight that the rest of the ward will be treated to a vista of exposed underwear when the carer moves to assist or hold a patient in bed. I like to wear earrings, and I have learned to wear only those that have no sharp bits, after a particularly tight and desperate hug from an unhappy person almost threatened to sever my jugular vein with the sharp metal edge of my earring.

Most of the encounters of the day bring little or no physical contact of any extensive nature: but the times when touch is required are urgent and important, and cannot be planned. Carers needs to know that if today is the day for holding a distraught and grieving person in their arms, that person will not get a black eye from a swinging necklace or tie pin as the carer bends closer, or a scratched face on a brooch or on zips set into breast pockets and sleeves. Also, it is more comfortable to be received into the arms of a soft jumper or tracksuit than those of a leather or tweed jacket.

The question of smell is also very important: we are not always aware of our own scents and odours, but we can be sure they are there. Clean clothes, body and hair are essential; so are clean teeth. It is a shame to put in front of a dying or bereaved person the additional hurdle of dealing with overpowering bad breath or body odour in the one who has to sit in very close proximity so as to listen to grief made indistinct by whispered words or weeping. Most days, in the work of spiritual care, you will not need your Bible or your prayer book: you will always need a bath, a reliable deodorant, and toothpaste.

One of the challenges of palliative care in an institutional setting (hospice, hospital or nursing home), is that good spiritual care takes into account the preferences of the individual, and since all individuals are different, some preferences are bound to conflict. The music that some patients in a ward find soothing and relaxing, others find irritating. The conversation and laughter that brings a sense of normality and comfort to one patient grates on the nerves of another. It is part of the task of spiritual care to try to balance and harmonize the given situation so that most people, if not all, feel that they have come to a place where they can relax, and trust enough to be themselves.

It is also helpful, where the budget and the building allow, to offer a variety of settings that will suit a variety of people (the London Lighthouse centre for people living with AIDS has done this most sensitively and creatively). In the hospice where I work, there are four-bedded bays, which can be very comforting to patients who are frightened of being alone but exhausting to those who prefer to be alone. There is a single room with obscured glass windows and an *en suite* lavatory, which some patients find a haven of privacy but others find isolating and claustrophobic. There is a double room, which has been a wonderful refuge for patients whose partners need to stay with them, but can be difficult when shared by two patients whose personalities are not entirely compatible. Spiritual care of the patient here lies in considering the needs of the patient in the context of their existing network of relationships, to offer the best option available for the needs of the individual. Also important is the acknowledgement of failure or insufficiency when the options available do not match the needs of the patient. To know that one's needs are seen and understood is helpful even if they cannot be met.

As well as the physical environment, attitude creates a powerful ambience. Lachrymose sympathy; brisk, relentless cheerfulness, patronizing and belittling speech and body language; baffling medical jargon that creates emotional distance and increases fear; obvious disapproval of a patient's lifestyle or personal relationships – these are the pitfalls.

Even more than the person who is dying, that person's partner or other loved ones can be intensely sensitive to body language and shades of meaning. In this time of emotional stress and weariness, offence is easily taken, and conclusions hastily reached. It is important for the spiritual care of all the people concerned that a good enough rapport is reached for misunderstandings to be untangled and communication to be maintained. The attitude which promotes good spiritual care is essentially uncondemning and accepting, so that fear and grief, helplessness and confusion can be admitted without the necessity for taking refuge in anger or withdrawal.

## PRAYER, CARE AND CONVERSATION

In the care of dying and bereaved people, an overlapping of prayer, care and conversation is necessary. The edges between these inevitably blur, and good teamwork is vital to facilitate this.

Thinking from the point of view of the spiritual work to be done, the time spent specifically on the most important pieces of spiritual work is almost in inverse proportion to its importance.

Spiritual achievement happens more by permission, by letting go, by trusting, than by effort. Often the real spiritual triumphs happen in a quiet moment set like a jewel in a supportive web of light-hearted chat, conversations on many topics, well-chosen medication and appropriate nursing care.

As the dying or bereaved people relax into an environment they recognize as trustworthy on all levels, and come to know the spiritual carers as comfortable friends, then the spiritual tasks can be addressed and allowed to emerge.

The issue of prayer is not straightforward. Many people welcome the comfort and peace of looking up to a higher being for comfort and strength, and are glad of someone to hold their hand and put into words their hopes and longings, their need for grace and support. But for some people, prayer can be embarrassing, or may be feared to signal 'the end', and is therefore a dread omen to be resisted.

Permission should always be sought, of course, before embarking on the saying of a prayer with anyone: spiritual beliefs are enormously varied, and the sharing of prayer can be offensive to some religious people, as well as to atheists.

Prayer can be a troubling issue for those spiritual carers who are people of religious faith working informally with a dying loved one – perhaps a partner bearing the main burden of nursing and spiritual care. For carers in this situation, there is the consideration of their own bereavement pain as their beloved dies, in addition to the demanding work of caring.

At such times, the carer often faces the additional stress of a feeling of spiritual block; a complete inability to pray. For a believer who understands the work of prayer to be an essential underpinning of the provision of spiritual care, this experience can be terribly distressing.

It may help, in preparation for such times, to enlarge our understanding of praying to go beyond the formulation of words.

Introducing other aspects of prayer, such as watching in prayer and praying action, can be very helpful. For a believer to recognize that God's presence is an unconditional grace, and simply to sit with the loved one, holding hands in wordless communion or gentle conversation, is a watching in prayer, a presentation of the self before the presence of healing grace that can ease the anxiety of the hopeless search for words. Most believers will be familiar with the idea of prophetic action: where the prophet may take an object like a stick or a pot, and carry out with it an action that has symbolic spiritual meaning. This idea can also be extended to the work of prayer, so that the carer can carry out the simple actions of emptying the commode, washing the dying person's face and keeping his/her mouth clean, monitoring the temperature of the room, all as a form of intercessory action, a direction of spiritual energy towards the creation of well-being, comfort and peace for the beloved being cared for. (See also Ch. 4, on religious tradition and the use of sacrament and symbol.)

Often, when it is dying, a cat will withdraw to a hidden and private place and make its end there. Many creatures seek privacy for those high holy moments of birth and death: they are momentous times, times whose reality engages with the core of our being, and so we are spiritually and emotionally very vulnerable, and can dread exposure, when we give birth and when we approach death. The bereaved as well as the dying stand on this exposed and vulnerable territory; it is of utmost importance to acknowledge and respect their need for privacy, and facilitate to the best of our ability their access to what constitutes privacy for them.

There are three main forms of privacy which it is important to ensure if we are to provide good spiritual care: physical privacy, manoeuvred privacy, and confidentiality.

The provision of physical privacy is one of the main indicators to a person of our sense of their dignity and worth. The more important people are, the more privacy they command: senior executives will have their own offices, juniors will not. The parents and oldest child of a family will probably have their own bedrooms; younger siblings are more likely to have to share. Sometimes we say of someone whose privacy is jealously guarded (as a GP's accessibility may be guarded by a receptionist), that 'It's like trying to get an audience with the Pope!' Whether we intend it or not, the privacy we offer people is a comment on the esteem and regard in which we hold them.

To be naked, to relieve bladder and bowels, to undergo medical examinations, all call for privacy to be given. And for most of us, most of the time, privacy is a gift given, not something we can ensure of ourselves: but this is especially true for people who are physically disabled or helpless. A severe source of stress for patients of nursing homes and psychiatric hospitals occurs when, in addition to the invasive interruptions of nursing routine, privacy is invaded by fellow-patients whose mental affliction has impaired or broken down completely their sense of appropriate barriers, and their ability to respect other people's space and territory.

The limitations of premises affect the amount of privacy it is possible to give. In a crowded hospital ward, or in the home of a sick person where the street door may open on the living room and the bathroom is out of reach upstairs, privacy may be hard to ensure. But the best that can be done should be done: using screens, a curtain round the bed, music to mask conversation – whatever is necessary.

In addition to physical privacy, the provision of what I have termed 'manoeuvred privacy' is most important. We speak of 'respecting' someone's privacy, and it is this sense of respect that will offer privacy even when the available premises limit the possibility of physical privacy considerably.

Privacy can be manoeuvred in several ways. A spiritual carer can, by the positioning of the chair at the bedside, or in relation to a patient's or bereaved person's seat in a day-care room or reception area, create the sense of a circle that excludes others, and thus offer privacy. Even a simple act like turning one's back, apparently engaging in something else, while a patient uses the commode, creates a sense of privacy.

Where the constant presence of visitors inhibits frank discussion of painful and intimate business, a carer can take opportunities to create one-to-one interviews ('Shall we go and have a cup of coffee together?') or arrange with other personnel on the care team to negotiate time alone, uninterrupted by visits.

Here again, it is most important that the members of the care team should recognize and support each other's work. It is disconcerting for a chaplain quietly saying the rosary with a dying patient to be assailed by a volunteer initiating a friendly chat about the weather, or for a carer sitting in silence with someone struggling to express hidden pain to deal with the invasion of a beautician breezily offering a manicure, which she would like to give *now*, as she is going home soon. Spiritual carers have to learn polite and assertive skills for heading off these interruptions; but the most delicate and significant interactions on spiritual ground are often shattered beyond recovery by insensitive interruptions.

Spiritual carers quickly learn that, when they do their work skilfully, they are often not perceived as doing any work at all. They often appear to be just chatting idly, or sitting quietly, because if they are working well the atmosphere will not be uncomfortably charged or forbidding, and other members of the care team will not be afraid of them, and so may hesitate less to interrupt them.

To manoeuvre privacy requires both skill and time. The drawing out of trust and the seizing of the right moment can only be done when there is time to watch and wait. Quality of spiritual care is inevitably sacrificed if there are too many people to see and too little time allowed.

As well as physical and manoeuvred privacy, there is no good spiritual care without the assurance of confidentiality. Secrets must remain secrets, and in an institutional setting there should be a clear understanding of what things will be shared among the care team and what will not. Of those things that are shared, the care team should be the absolute boundary of the information. Reliable confidentiality is the foundation of trust.

## HUMOUR

Death, dying and disability can give rise to humour (I have tried to think of a way of putting this that doesn't sound in *very* poor taste, and I can't think of one). Wit, laughter and banter are wise ways of drawing the sting of fear and indignity. It is when people trust each other, when the one dying or bereaved and the companions on the journey have established a good rapport and understanding, that humour which might otherwise offend becomes a grace.

Sometimes also, the situations that arise carry their own extraordinary comedy. I recall one story told by a man who sat by the bedside of a very sick friend in a small four-bed ward in the hospice. The sick man's partner was also there. In the bed opposite, another man lay dying. The breathing of the dying man had moved into noisy Cheyne-Stokes breathing, and the mood of the ward was very quiet, somewhat oppressed by the sense of death being very near. Perhaps in an effort to alleviate the atmosphere, someone had turned on the television, and a children's cartoon programme, *The Animals of Farthing*

*Wood*, was being broadcast. This programme tells the story of a variety of animals undertaking a journey together, and the interaction between them and the other animals they meet. Some of the animals are predators, some would normally be prey, and occasionally mistakes occur, as in this particular episode. Into the tense and solemn atmosphere of the hospice ward, as visitors and patients sat in quietness while death approached, one of the cartoon characters announced with some emotion: 'I'm *terribly* sorry – oh, I'm so embarrassed – I don't know how to tell you this, but I've *eaten* your *wife!*'

This bizarre and surreal experience still reduces the men who were there that night to helpless laughter as they tell the story.

Such moments come with even greater impact because of the emotional tension they break.

Another story I recall is about a very sick man, drifting in and out of consciousness, but still at that stage receiving his medicines orally, and capable of taking a little food. Late one evening, as the nurses came round with the drugs trolley, his partner tried to take advantage of the tail-end of a more wakeful spell to coax him to eat the dessert he had requested and to take his medicines. I recall very vividly the blend of humour and tenderness in that coaxing: 'Do you want your trifle now? Can you open your eyes for me? Are you awake enough for your drugs? Drugs? Trifle? Drugs and trifle? Does that sound good – drugs and trifle? Tell you what, I'll have the drugs, you have the trifle. This is a good party.'

Watching, listening, it makes you smile, and it breaks your heart.

## 3

# *A Trinity of Presence*

SPEECH AND SILENCE

Silence is often presented as the absence of speech, when speech is seen to be communication, relationship. In such an understanding, silence is the moment in which one is 'robbed of speech', has 'nothing to say', when 'words failed me'. Is it like that?

It may be looked at in another way. Maybe silence is naked, intense communication. Maybe words clothe the nakedness of being that is revealed in silence. Maybe silence forces into view the self that would rather have taken refuge in the exchange of words, the easier currency of conversation.

Or perhaps it is just a question of appropriateness; a time to speak, and a time to keep silence.

But whichever it is, it is important for the spiritual carer, in the sensitive, delicate handling of the accompanying of dying and bereaved people on their journey, to know how to use both words and silence wisely. Words are empty and meaningless when the companionship of silence is needed. Silence is felt as an oppression and a threat when one is longing for the comfort and reassurance of conversation.

In keeping company with one who is dying or holding the agony of loss, the whole range of communication may be experienced – words, silence, touch – and carers must learn above all else to fine-tune their sensitivity, to feel a way into the language of the one they are accompanying, so as to respond appropriately, to allow the meeting of souls which assuages loneliness and permits healing, freedom and peace to come.

To ignore simple social courtesies with a person just because she/he is dying or bereaved would be disrespectful. To introduce oneself, to offer a cup of tea, to remark on the weather, to pay a compliment on a person's clothes or hair, to discuss holidays and families and makes of car and gardening:

such conversation enables the person to get a feeling about the carer, to decide whether this is someone to place trust in. It also gives the carer a sense of the wholeness of the personality being cared for: how disrespectful it would be to brush aside these idiosyncratic elements of someone's life as irrelevant in the face of death. Even in the last days of life, the small change of the social currency of conversation can be an anchoring, comforting thing. In bereavement it can provide a buffer against pain, a breathing space in torment. Many bereaved people use light small talk as a way of spacing agony, a way of making manageable the task of facing up to unbearable loss.

But it should not be all chit-chat. The carer may talk about, or be invited to talk about, deeper things. Usually this happens gracefully, easily. For example, in a hospital ward, the carer might comment on the lovely sunshine, and the flowers growing outside the ward window, then ask if the patient has a garden at home. Conversation can then naturally explore the subject of home, the pain of being away from home, the dread of losing home altogether, the sadness of selling up and going into a nursing home. If that is enough to face for now, there are the flowers outside the ward window providing an escape route for the conversation. But if the opportunity to talk has been longed for, this might be the time for anguish to be shared and fear confessed.

If the conversation does move in deeper at this point, sooner or later silence will be entered, like wandering unexpectedly into a glade in a wood. Silence, suddenly opening out around us, not just a gap or an interlude, but a real place of its own. Good spiritual care rests easy with such silence, permits the momentousness of its presence, the intimacy of its stillness, the deep, unspoken exchanges that take place there.

I remember an extraordinary place of silence I came into with a hospice patient in the last days of his life. I had offered to say a prayer with him. He had been a church-goer, but not an especially religious man. I held his hand and said a simple prayer, and as we continued to sit in the silence that followed, something amazing happened. I felt it physically; it was like being carried in a swelling sea, a movement and lift of waves, a tremendous spiritual power, an intensification of reality, as though we had been caught up in the tide of life itself. It was awesome. Holy. From time to time he whispered, in amazement and wonder, 'I don't deserve it. I don't deserve it.' For almost an hour we were caught up in it, and then it was gone. Windsurfing on silence is one of the rare privileges of spiritual care.

In their understanding of spiritual things, people differ in their experience of the silence of God, just as they vary in their experience of silence between people. Just as there are people who cannot bear the quiet that sometimes falls between people as conversation drifts and dies, so there are people who are disturbed and even enraged by the silence of God. For them it may be a sign of absence or indifference, and they conclude that God is cold, either because God is dead or because God does not care. It is not like that for everyone. Some people find God's silence to have its own speech: for them the divine stirs as wisdom, direction, words of strength and peace. And then there are the one or two who gaze into the silence of God as a lover loses himself in the eyes of the beloved: in their souls God's silence is written as a love letter; and to such people others find their way hungry, for those are the ones whose presence brings healing and peace.

But, *when* to speak? Perhaps a good rule of thumb is that it is all right for the patient to be afraid of silence, but not the carer. Sometimes patients have said to me, 'Talk to me. Don't just sit there quietly. Say something.' And that is the time to use intuition; to talk comfortably about whatever may seem to help the patient, whether that be the supper menu or one's own experience of deep loss, whatever feels right. But the carer must always be alert for the moment the patient needs to talk or to re-enter silence, alert for the need for self-effacement again.

And then there is the matter of weighing up when to go; of discerning the difference between a silence of completion and a silence weighty with things needing to be gently explored.

The key to it lies in realizing that silence is a language, as full of communication and information as words are. A silence is to be read, heard, beheld. Silence is deeper, more transformative than words. But both are necessary, for silence is arrived at through words, and words find their value in silence.

31

## THE LITURGY OF TOUCH

The silence of God is mediated to us by words. By the word of Scripture, the words of prayers and poetry, we sketch God's outline. Our adoration, petition and praise crayon in the page, and where the colours leave off, the white radiance of a shape emerges – something, Someone – someone who is elusive and strange, whom all our words fail to capture, yet someone whose shape we might never have discerned without the pattern of prayer and praise.

We are used to liturgy as a web of words, a sacred dance celebrating and embodying the being of the holy, channelling to us an experience of grace. Touch is also holy. Touch directly, dynamically, powerfully communicates good or evil intention. Touch is brutal, gentle, healing, coercive: it is raw language, immediate communication, spirit unmixed with water. Touch can bypass the muddle of words. For the agnostic, the atheist, the person of faith traditionally at loggerheads with our own faith, touch can be a means of sharing grace without the weariness of negotiation or the fear of compromise.

Many people, asking or permitting me to say a prayer with them, will as a matter of course hold my hand while we pray. Our joined hands, the unity of our touch, form the temple of the presence of the holy. And more often than not, as the words of the prayer end, we rest together in silence, simply holding hands, and our touch is a deeper prayer than our words.

Sometimes I will bless someone who is dying with a form of words, and by making a sign of the cross on the forehead. Sometimes I will hold in my arms someone who is sobbing in a torment of grief. Sometimes I will put out my hand and lightly touch the arm of someone who needs a little reassurance. And no doubt I sometimes get it wrong, since the risk attached to doing anything is always greater than the risk of doing nothing.

I find a priestly aspect in the rôle of spiritual carer. As I introduce myself to a new patient in the hospice – 'Hello, I'm Pen, the Free Church Chaplain' – I am introducing myself as a representative of the Church, even of God. From that moment on, whether I like it or not, what I am, how I am, who I am, preaches. I become a sort of acted parable. If God is the God who touches people, who bends down and lightly kisses the cheek of a dying woman, who sits by the bedside of a blind and paralysed man, holding his hand – well, maybe they will want to get acquainted with that God.

The inevitable question is: What about those who find touch invasive, unwelcome? The answer to that is easy enough to say, but requires skill and sensitivity to practise. It is simply that we have to expand our concept of language so that we hear, read, speak with our bodies as confidently as we do with our words. If we understand the signals of a person's posture and gesture, we will know how close to come, how much space to give, when a touch needs to be finger-light, firm, enfolding.

Touch can have a function of re-earthing people, of re-connecting them to themselves. Sometimes the experience of grief is like being cast adrift, lost. Words then can be ex-perienced as meaningless, puzzling and alien, increasing the sense of estrangement, and that is frightening. Touch often re-establishes a sense of being and self, relocating us in the here and now. So it functions as a creator of continuity.

Sometimes touch may be needed to create a continuum between the past and the present. When a loved one has just died, the one left behind may need the carer to be there, holding hands with the two of them (the one who is bereaved, and the one who has died). When someone has died, it may be important to offer a gentle caress, a kiss on the brow, holding and stroking his/her hand, so that the terror of death and the sense of separation are softened for the ones left behind, and there is no whiff of horror or uncleanness in the presence of that beloved body.

Liturgy is often thought of as essentially a ritual – a ritualization of our experience of sacredness. It can also be thought of as a container; a silver bowl left under a waterfall, a specific time and place that captures something of the bright flowing of the holy. Touch becomes liturgy when it is like that. God is the ground and source and ultimacy of reality: God is not the projection of religious concepts and images, but is greater and deeper and nearer and more wonderful than that. When, in the moments beyond words – moments of tears or of wonder or of deepest need – we reach out for another human being and that touch becomes grace for us, lovingly, faithfully reconnects us with at least some semblance of reality, then touch has become liturgy, capturing something of the bright flowing of the holy.

## PHYSICAL CLOSENESS – NON-INVASION, INTIMACY AND RISK

Many people have a dread of offering inappropriate touch – or for that matter, of saying the wrong thing – and the less relaxed about it one becomes, the easier it is to get it wrong. Perhaps because the language of touch is more powerful than words, inappropriate touch seems an even more crashing error than the wrong words. But is it so awful, to get it wrong, to misunderstand or run the risk of being misunderstood? The person who hugs everyone is probably being insensitive to some people's signals. So is the person who hugs no one.

Part of the fear of getting it wrong lies in the need on the part of professionals to maintain correctness as a sign of their superiority. To get it wrong is humiliating for a professional carer, and in the language of touch which magnifies and intensifies all communication, the risk of getting it wrong is increased. So professional carers often shy away from touch. Anxiety desensitizes one to other people's needs, so it is probably a good thing for those carers who feel anxious about touch to use its language with caution. Likewise, one should heed comments from others: colleagues do not lightly say, 'Your touch is inappropriate. You touch too much. They don't like it,' and, therefore, such warnings should be considered seriously. But other than that, carers can rest easy in the knowledge that nobody gets it right all of the time: it is all right not to be perfect, it is okay to make mistakes.

In meetings of professional carers where touch is discussed, the patient's vulnerability is often mentioned, and the topic is often considered as though the patient could approach touch only subjectively, whereas the carers were at all times cool and objective in their approach. Everybody knows this is not really true, but a certain amount of 'let's pretend' takes place, around the understanding that the carer's self is adequately masked or contained by the rôle of professional carer, whereas the rôle of patient allows freedom to be a human being. In actual fact, patients are often acting more in accordance with their interpretation of the rôle of 'patient' than is recognized, and carers are often less in control of their own human responses than they like to acknowledge.

A serious disadvantage of this discreet 'let's pretend' is that too often the carer *hides* behind a mask of professionalism, shifting responsibility to the patient for the carer's responses. For example, if a patient is suffering from unmet needs – loneliness, perhaps – the carer will probably pick this up intuitively. Carers generally have an idea of themselves as givers, 'nice guys', and may feel ashamed and guilty that they are not prepared to extend their professional relationship with the patients to offer the friendship that they need to assuage their loneliness. If carers feel uncomfortable and unwilling to look at their own sense of shame and guilt that is thus aroused, a simple way of dealing with it is to maintain an imperturbable professional face and offer a judgement that 'this patient is very manipulative'.

Likewise, the honesty of 'I can't stand that bloody woman – she grates on my nerves' is often presented as a more poised and objective judgement that the patient under question has – or is – a problem.

And everybody knows that it must not be true that carers may find some situations or people difficult to deal with, since it implies a compromising and unevenness of the quality of care. And since it must not be true, it is most often dealt with as if it were not true: carers, like everybody else, are ultimately more interested in professional survival than personal honesty. 'The Emperor has no clothes' is bound to be an unpopular observation in a multi-disciplinary case-conference!

In interacting with people who are dying and newly bereaved, however, one stands on holy ground: one stands in a place of truth and reality, where life demands more of naked self and less of smooth technique than most professional situations require. To bring dishonesty into holy ground is to play a very dangerous game indeed, for it requires a detachment from integrity which is spiritually disabling. Not only that, but dishonesty communicates powerfully through touch and other body language. On observing unacknowledged fear and dishonesty in a carer, a patient will often gently withdraw from the demanding and momentous interpersonal work that is required to achieve real spiritual peace. One of the saddest failures of palliative care is when a human being has died, quietly relinquishing his or her own accomplishment of the spiritual journey because the carer would not admit that being the companion on that journey was simply too demanding.

In an ideal world there would be someone – whether a friend or a professional – with whom every carer felt it safe to be completely honest: someone to whom it was possible to admit the cost and the risk and the vulnerability of holy ground; its extraordinary intimacy, its emotional power. Too often, however, the carer's world is fraught with taboos which make it hard to admit to having a normal human response without losing face.

Any counselling course deals with the issue of touch, and always in terms of warning. The vulnerability of the patient/ client is stressed, and the danger that need may transform into a sexual fixation on the carer/counsellor/minister. Mention is often made of the dangers of counselling the opposite sex (there is a kind of arrogance here: one should not make assumptions about a patient's sexual orientation). At its grimmest, a recommendation may be made that touch be restricted to light hand contact with a place on the centre of the patient's back.

Certainly it pays to learn about touch. Ultimately, however, the best way is not to contain it with prohibitions that tinge touching with shame. The best way is to learn to read its language, and prohibitions and inhibitions hinder that process severely.

In learning the language of touch, the first step is acknowledgement. It is not always good to act on instinct or desire, but it always pays to acknowledge it.

If you meet someone from whose touch you recoil, don't tell yourself off; ask yourself why, and bear it in mind for future reference. It may be that the person needs to be touched if they are grieving, lonely or afraid. Stay in contact with your own feelings of reticence, however: it might be something simple; perhaps they smell bad or remind you of someone you don't like. Your own responses need not block you from showing gentleness and compassion, but stay in contact with instinctual warning signals. Your touch will carry its own messages of reticence, and this will place its own limits on the encounter. But do not be afraid to withdraw tactfully from relationships in which you feel you are out of your depth; you are unlikely to do good healing work if all your own alarm systems are jangling. Carers should work in teams, so that appropriate matching up of patient and carer can happen.

Again, you may find you have a very warm response to some patients or bereaved people. Here the task is to continue gently effacing yourself, making no emotional demands, not laying down foundations of friendship, but continuing in a professional relationship until your work together is done. After that time has passed, the time for friendship may come. Effacing oneself and making no emotional demands does not mean that you have to pretend to yourself that you respond to everyone the same, that there is no special rapport. It is there. Just hold it, be grateful for it, but do not take advantage of it. It is abusive when a carer uses patients to gratify his or her own emotional needs, but it is not abusive to have an emotional response.

Of course the great area of shame is sex. An inappropriate sexual response generates great shame and confusion. There is no real need to get more worked up about this than about any other inappropriate responses, however. The same rule applies: watch it, acknowledge it, and do not allow it to become coercive or abusive. If it is the patient's response to you, deal with it gently, but make your position clear. If it is your response, acknowledge it but do not act on it: and probably it would be wiser to pass that patient on to someone else's care.

It should not need saying, but it does, that because this area of pastoral work is emotionally highly charged and intense, all spiritual carers should have a means of fulfilling and meeting their own sexual, emotional and physical needs. Nobody should rely on terminally ill people and their grieving relatives to meet his/her need for physical and emotional affirmation. Friends and sexual partners are the appropriate people for that. It is very, very helpful to have one or two people with whom it is possible to be absolutely open about one's self; someone who will not raise an eyebrow or purse their lips or send any messages to reinforce shame and self-doubt.

All human beings, however unruffled their surface, are elemental, turbulent beings; helpless in desire, in longing, in the yearning to be loved and held and known. This is a matter for rejoicing; it is what it means to be made in the image of God. But the power and energy of our needs and desires must be dealt with in other ways than by foisting them inappropriately on to other people, be that openly or under the guise of a professional interaction.

Really, the way forward is not to step up the caution, but to learn to trust, to leave fear behind. Take risks in your private life; risk being honest, putting into words your feelings, your shame, your need. Then the grey world of subterfuge and twisted need in which inappropriate touch flourishes will lessen its hold.

## A SPACE FOR TEARS

Perhaps one of the rarest and most useful things one can offer a person who is dying or bereaved is a space for tears; someone with whom it is safe to cry, one who is not embarrassed or alarmed by someone else's tears.

Very often, when I am with a person who has been recently bereaved, the swelling of anguish inside them overflows in tears. And very often, as they begin to cry, they say, 'I'm sorry.'

The reasons for the apology vary with the individual.

Some are embarrassed by the admission of weakness. Very often, still, men are brought up with the maxim, repeatedly reinforced, that it is unmanly to cry, that a man should be able to contain his emotion without breaking down into tears. There are many women, too, whose upbringing requires that in the company of other people they should be composed and calm; for them the disorder of weeping is a failure of self-control, a matter of shame.

Some, and these are usually women, who are alongside a loved friend who is dying, try not to cry because they want to show a bright and happy face to their beloved one. For these people, the weakness of tears is interpreted as placing an emotional burden on the one who is dying. They feel that, in these last days or weeks, they must allow the one dying to be weak, and must be strong for him/her.

Connected with this is the anxiety in some women about spoiling their appearance. Sometimes an immaculate turn-out is the shell of protection they have pulled around the agony of the wounded heart. A red and blotchy face running with mascara makes that inner agony apparent on the outside, leaving them more vulnerable than feels bearable.

Some have shouldered a rôle of being the strong and stoical one for the rest of the bereaved people: 'the man of the house', 'the mother of the family'. 'My children never saw me cry' can be the one triumph wrested from an experience of crucifying pain.

And there are those who have been forbidden to cry. Nurses trained by people who had little emotional insight often report experiences from early days of training when they were sharply and traumatically reprimanded for weeping at the death or suffering of a patient.

I remember with a wrench of sadness one nurse who told the story of her mother's death. She had nursed her mother, putting aside her own feelings of helpless grief to offer her skills as a tender gift of practical love. Her own pain was put on hold. Then her mother told her that she was not to cry after her (the mother's) death. 'You mustn't cry for me.' And her daughter never did cry for her: because she loved her, because she wouldn't betray her by not keeping faith with those stupid, selfish instructions. When she speaks of it, plain in her face is written the profound sadness of unshed tears; but she will not let them fall.

I have seen men at the funerals of their wives, exhorted by their relatives, 'Come on, chin up! It doesn't suit you to have your chin down!' and, 'Think of the others. Think of your brothers and sisters.'

Good spiritual care offers a space for tears – holds back those clamouring voices, makes a way through for dammed up grief to be released, the burden to be laid down.

There is no 'ought to' about weeping. From time to time I meet bereaved people, and people who are accompanying dying friends on their journey, who express frustration and re-sentment at the well-meant advice of acquaintances and health professionals who say to them, 'You ought to cry. You need to cry.' Some people in grief and anguish cannot bear to cry. There are some, particularly those in real agony of bereavement, for whom the pain is too much to be expressed in weeping. These people have to hold still, have to be motionless and mute, in order to contain the agony of grief that is tearing them apart inside. Again, there are some whose natural response to emotional pain is to withdraw, to enter a spiritual winter, still and cold, watching and waiting, enduring, reflecting the stature of death in their dignified and quiet bearing. For such people, tears will come, but another time, in another way: perhaps at an anniversary when the pain is still raw but no longer overwhelming; perhaps in private, after the death and the funeral, when the business is complete – then may be the time for tears to flow. Good spiritual care does not *instruct* people to weep; but it makes a space for tears.

This cannot be done without time. The carer must give the time that is needed for the one in grief to find the courage, take the risk, of articulating and exposing private pain. A carer's spirituality at this time must be as wide and kind and self-effacing as the sky, providing a background and a context, accepting and permitting the grief to be expressed. Tears that heal come when one trusts enough to relax, when one can allow the wound to be seen, touched, heard, by a gentle other.

## LISTENING – YOU, ME AND GOD, A TRINITY OF PRESENCE

All this is accomplished by the art of pastoral listening. Pastoral listening has other dimensions than conversational or educational listening; it involves attending to several levels at once.

The simplest element of listening is that of attending to another's words (and even that is not done accurately by many). Words themselves operate on different planes of meaning. For example, the restless patient who talks of getting ready for a journey – 'I must get my tickets. I must get my papers in order' – may be confused, may be reliving old memories, or may be communicating a coded expression of the need to prepare for death. And in the case of those who are confused or reliving old memories, there will be something about their present situation which evokes a connection; there will be resonances with reality in what they have to say – they will be telling their story precisely, even if they are not presenting accurate facts. It is always worth attending to and pondering on another's choice of words, and hearing their story. To be really heard is a rare luxury for many people.

But we listen with our eyes as well as our ears. Gesture, degree of animation, all the rich vocabulary of body language, will tell the carer as much as words do and more. The clenched fist, the little frown of anxiety, the averted eyes, the vulnerable, horrified mouth; these will alert our listening eyes to pain that needs to be reached, acknowledged, touched.

Sometimes too we listen with our whole bodies. The person who finds a place to weep in our arms and clings in abandoned weeping; we listen with our bodies for the relaxing, the withdrawing, the diminishing of the storm; we hear when it is time to sit back, to let go, gently to move on.

Listening needs stamina. Spiritual carers each have their own saturation point. Absorbing others' pain is costly, and each of us learns to be familiar with our own limits in listening. In pastoral listening, however, there is a kind of listening which is very valuable for those who spend day after day hearing and responding to others' pain. It is a sort of still, meditative listening that requires the carer to remain centred in oneself without becoming exhausted by the minutiae of the other's history.

To listen like this, the carer does not take on board the facts, the information, that the patient is pouring out; rather, the carer listens to the patient as a *person*, discovering the vibrations of that person on the sensitive interface of the two personalities. Carers keep in touch with what is aroused in their own being by the patient's being. They note each changing or dominant vibration, and then let it go, staying with the flow. Anger, tension, weariness, sadness – they experience the sense of these as they arise, evoked by the being of the patient, and respond to these, rather than to the information the patient is communicating. Thus they might feed back, 'You seem to feel very angry about that,' or, 'I feel a real sadness when you share that with me,' rather than saying, 'Did he? That was an awful thing to do!' or, 'And what did you do next?'

Interestingly, although what is apparently the substance of the communication (the words or the information contained in them) is less responded to than their emotional content, this kind of listening often brings great relief, enabling the patient to feel that his/her *self* has been heard; and that is what the need is. Further, it is a form of listening which is less exhausting for the listener, who can remain centred and still in their own equilibrium, rather than roller-coastering up and down the patient's experiences.

This ability to remain poised, centred, collected as a listener is an important skill for the spiritual carer; for spiritual care embraces another dimension than the psychological (though undoubtedly psychology enters the picture).

When we listen, we can be a bridge, a touching place, a way back into spiritual connectedness for the one who is torn apart by grief or fear. If we do not allow ourselves to be dragged here and there by the patient's experiences and responses, but in simplicity remain present, centred, then we may become like a rock in a turbulent river; an earthed solidity, a connection with the ground of being, a place of respite.

In so doing one remembers the presence of God in listening, giving tangible form to the steadiness and patience of the God-who-is-there, the God who is peace, who is with us.

Often such listening is all that is required to give the patient confidence (con-fidence means 'with-faith') to re-establish their own spirituality, to find, amid the fragments of life as it was, at least a small spring of grace, a hope of meaning.

# 4

## The Dancing Chameleon

### THE HABITS OF A LIFETIME

The time of dying is often a time for asking old questions long shelved, and for finally addressing unfinished business: it is unlikely to be the time for trying something completely new. Often new projects are undertaken – swimming with the dolphins or a wonderful holiday – which uplift and nourish the spirit. But these new projects are likely to be in keeping with the established character of the person. When people are dying, to themselves they often feel diminished and altered, less than the people they were. Sometimes relatives and friends see them that way too, especially if there is loss of physical substance; hair loss or considerable weight loss. And yet often in dying, the core personality asserts itself more strongly than ever. It is often a time when the flame of the self burns more intensely despite losing physical ground.

There are times in life, and dying and bereavement are such times, when choices have to be made and preferences become clear; it is in such choices that the self is seen.

In the terminal phase of illness, body systems close down, and a person's world contracts. The outer circle of personal acquaintances are not wanted any more. Only the care team and the dying person's dearest ones have a place here. This can be very painful for visitors who must be turned away. Relationships that have survived a long time on pretence now may become apparent for what they are.

Spiritually, the orientation of the self becomes clearer too. Some people adamantly refuse to see a chaplain: without the energy for politeness or social form, they turn their faces now from religion which for them engendered only anger or fear.

Others ask to see a chaplain, wanting an opportunity for a formal peacemaking with God, the ritual salving and shriving of the soul. Others seek assistance to address spiritual issues, not by means of religious ritual, but by talking and sharing ideas. But whatever that person's way of approaching spirituality has been, that is the way they are likely to choose now, or the way they will instinctively return to.

It is helpful for anyone accompanying them on this way of the spirit to know where their path comes from. A spiritual carer can probably be of better assistance by knowing where someone has come from than by having strongly formed opinions as to where they are going. To know that someone has been a Buddhist or an atheist or a Jew is more useful than knowing that one would like to say a prayer with him/her.

When people have to leave their own homes and come into institutional care, good spiritual care should allow religious or ideological observance to continue. Some ideologies, such as veganism or macrobiotics, are philosophies extending to the whole way of life, but have particular dietary implications, as do many religions. Christians have no dietary regulations, so if the only spiritual carer available is the Church of England chaplain, then it will help if he/she is knowledgeable about and sympathetic to the requirements and practices of other faiths and ideologies.

The provision of good spiritual care requires a curiosity to see the world from another's point of view, and sensitivity to trace the thread of an individual's habits of worship and spirituality, so as to accompany others on the paths of their own choosing, and work within their own frameworks.

### EMPATHY

In my own work accompanying dying people on their journeys, and bereaved people on theirs, I find myself again and again using particular skills, to the end of helping them find the confidence to appropriate the peace life offers them.

First is the willingness to empathize. Watching and listening with hungry intensity, I have tried to absorb into every surface of being and sensitivity all that emanates from the person I am with: the look on the face, the turn of the head, the laughter lines around the eyes, the little frown of stress, the brief catching breath of pain. To read the being of another person is like reading a novel: tone of voice and body language yielding a story, a mythology, an unfolding tale or map.

44

And with some people it can be more like reading the stars, or reading the tea-leaves, a highly interpretative, intuitive, chancy skill.

I have often heard people react with anger to being told by others, 'I understand,' or 'I know just how you feel.' Such well-meant insensitivity compromises the sense of aloneness that belongs to suffering, presumes to violate the privacy of the wounded animal's lair. One should not be so rash and patronizing as to say, 'I understand.' One should always carry in mind that this is holy ground, where one is privileged to stand in the sanctuary of the other's humanity, and not dare to assert an 'I' into the other's atmosphere of spirit. But just to shrug the shoulders and *not* understand won't do either. One must lovingly learn the other person like a beloved symphony or play; until one can feed back or mirror, can transmit not the egocentric, 'I understand,' but the more self-effacing, 'I have heard you. I have seen you.' That brings comfort, but it stands at a little distance, accords the other the centrality on their appointed holy ground.

This work of empathizing is totally absorbing: even a little unbalancing! At times, I find myself living in, radiating, the attitudes of the one I am accompanying, trying out in my own being the existential orientations I have sensed in them. When I am engaged in this work, the most difficult task of all is to have to leave the presence of the one I am accompanying to fulfil other duties, especially to attend social functions which require light-hearted and superficial interpersonal exchange. I know of nothing more difficult than leaving a vigil of hours at the side of a dying person in his/her last hours to go to a sherry party. It gives a sense of recalling the soul with massive effort from far away and deep, recalling it to the garish light of pointless social antics, requiring oneself to turn away from the centre of the universe to the frill on the outmost periphery. It is an odd thing that parties, laughter and get-togethers are thought to vibrate with life, while hospice wards supposedly reverberate with the fear of death. I do not find it so. The butterfly world of gin and tonic and polite laughter, the mendacious cries of, 'That would be lovely!' and 'How nice to meet you!', can feel like death's creatures of ephemerality and emptiness. The bedside of a quiet room, silent except for the labour of breathing, charged with worlds of sadness, loving, tenderness, turmoil, peace: to be there is to venture upon the place of life's fountain-head, to look life in the eyes and find meaning.

Empathy, then, is a demanding, utterly absorbing enterprise. A little like meditation, it requires that one make another the focus, for a while, of all one's being. To do this means that one will love them. It is costly, therefore. Yet empathy has also to be balanced with the ability to keep a core of detachment at the centre. One has to be always the listener, the observer; there has to be a certain coldness, a disunion, in order for empathy to happen; otherwise one will simply paint one's own values, needs and emotions over the canvas of the other life, obscuring the other's reality with one's own. The art of self-effacement is a necessary skill for companions on this journey; even sometimes to the danger-point of forgetting and being unable to find one's own self again. It is, therefore, important in this work to have a loyal circle of loved personal friends, whose affection helps one to re-earth, to relocate the self which has been abdicated in favour of treading another's path.

Holding in balance these arts of losing oneself in another while retaining a dispassionate, observing eye is a necessary skill for this work.

SPIRITUAL LINGUISTICS

Another helpful skill is what I have come to call 'spiritual linguistics'.

All societies are shared by those who dominate and those who are subject, the powerful and the oppressed, the ruling class and the serving class. The serving class invariably knows much more about the society as a whole than the ruling class does. This is because, in order to survive, those of the serving class have to learn not only their own language, but that of the ruling class as well. They have to sharpen their powers of observation in order to be able to react acutely and appropriately to the other. Those whose job requires skills of shrewd and accurate observation can do no better than to spend time with the groups of people who suffer prejudice, rejection, marginalization and subordination. The very survival of such people depends on the acuteness of their insight, their ability to predict how the other will react, their ability to adapt to a world not their own. The legendary intelligence and ability to succeed of Jewish people, the extraordinary sensitivity of homosexual men, are in part due to this: nothing sharpens the wits like persecution. Patients everywhere concur in their opinion that it is the nurse, not the doctor, who can detect when the time of dying has come; who can sense how the patient 'is', beyond the weighing of the clinical data. That is because in a medical environment the doctor is at the pinnacle of the power heap; this in itself, whatever the occupational acumen, will disable the power of insight.

To offer good spiritual care, the carer must master the art of spiritual linguistics; the art of being able to speak to the other intelligibly.

To be a chaplain in a highly charged emotional environment, such as a hospice sometimes is, one must be something of a dancing chameleon, taking on the colour and shading of others' worlds, able to move lightly into and out of the linguistic modes of doctors and nurses, of patients, with their varying backgrounds, upbringing and occupational training, and the loved ones of those patients, the varying dynamics of relational networks. By body language, by tone of voice, by the sensitivity to judge a moment – when to say nothing, when to touch, when to make a joke – by facial expression, a carer must communicate what should never be said; 'I understand.'

To understand is not to replicate another's experience – that cannot be done – but to learn another's language, both phraseology and gesture, and to reply in kind.

A friend told me recently of her experience in accompanying a family with a genetic disorder to a London hospital, to learn from the consultant there about the problem that was afflicting, or carried by, several family members. My friend observed that the family were overawed by the environment and the doctor, and that he spoke to them swiftly and concisely, using medical terms beyond their comprehension. He asked if they had any questions. They said they had not, not because they now understood, but because they knew they would not understand the answers. They came home still ignorant about the implication for their family of their genetic problem.

There were two possibilities there. Either the family could become, in their own time, informed about the illness, the terms related to it, and the phrases, jargon and abbreviations of the medical world. They could also learn middle-class phraseology, body language and verbal modes, and familiarize themselves with the different aspects of educational and social background that shaped the doctor's language. Then they would understand him.

Alternatively, the doctor could read their signs of confusion, hear the uncertainty in their voices, the unease of their demeanour, and realize that their vocabulary and modes of expression were not consistent with his. He could learn to hear and see those signs of bafflement and sense of inferiority common to all humanity. He could ask them to explain in their own words exactly what they understood about their genetic disorder. Then he would have understood them. He could then proceed to choose words from their vocabulary, phrased in sentences consistent with the kind they used, presented in body language appropriate for their need to be made at home, reassured, relaxed. Then they would have understood him (and he could double-check to make sure they had).

It is the person who takes on the responsibility for the success of the communication who provides the spiritual care in any situation. In this case, it was my friend: she asked the doctor questions in his communicational mode, and explained the answers to the family in theirs when they got home.

People are made by God in God's image. They are all spiritual – 'little lower than the angels' as the psalm says. They do not need to be given a spiritual journey or made into spiritual beings; all that is part of what they are already. What they need is someone who can 'speak their language', who can enter their mode of communication with enough authenticity to reassure them that they are not strangers, they are not alone. To reassure someone that they can make themselves understood when they share themselves with you is a different thing from insisting that you understand. The only times 'I understand' has to be said are the times when it is not true. People know who understands them; it is the people who speak their language who

understand them. Spiritual linguistics is a fundamental skill of
spiritual care.

## THE POWER OF SACRAMENT AND SYMBOL

John Wesley asserted that the sacrament of Holy Communion
was a 'converting ordinance'. The Church's traditional definition of a sacrament is that it is 'an outward and visible sign of
an inward and invisible grace'. Different denominations of the
Church disagree as to how many sacraments there are – two?
five? seven? – but all agree that the sacraments are a centre,
focus or magnet for numinous experience, a meeting-point with
the holy.

Sacraments are about supreme reality. They bring into flesh
the world of the spirit; make concrete concepts that cannot
be pinned down into words. It is interesting that the two
sacraments – baptism and Communion – that all the Christian
denominations agree upon who have any sacramental theology
at all, are intensely reliant upon multi-sensory symbols in
their enactment. Bread and wine; the action of tearing apart
the rough bread, the smooth fire of wine on the tongue, its
connection with the tearing open of a life, the flow of life-blood,
the central conceptual connection of nourishing and breaking
down, of nurturing and dying, and all this in the fellowship
circle of a meal.

Without words, it is all there, there for the blind or the deaf
as for the sighted and hearing, for those of intellect and those
whose understanding is simple. The wordless act embodies the
central grace: the words merely enshrine the tradition and tell
the story. And that story-telling also has power; the repetition
going back hundreds of years, the quiet voice rehearsing the
story – 'in the same night that he was betrayed, he took bread,
and broke it, and gave it to his disciples saying . . .' The power
is in the familiarity.

For Christian believers nearing death, and for their loved
ones, the familiar words and familiar actions have a quiet
power and a very healing and reassuring effect. They gently
assert a continuity, for one thing; that this thing which believers
have done for hundreds of years – in magnificent cathedrals,
in war-time trenches, in country chapels – will continue as it

does today as long as the human story continues. In that sense of continuity, there is a sense of being carried; of being, even in one's weakness, part of an indomitable, enduring, unforgettable tradition; of belonging to Jesus, who also died, and who offers the grace of risen life. But as well as the tradition, there is in that sacrament an expression of fundamental reality for people who are facing death: 'The Lord Jesus, in the same night he was betrayed, took bread, and broke it, and gave it to his disciples, saying, "This is my body . . ."'

People who are facing death and grief understand the symbolism of night, 'the night when he was betrayed' – they know what it means to be betrayed; to be let down by their bodies, to live in a world no longer reliable, to feel life itself turn its back on them. They know that dark night of betrayal which is encountered in helplessness; and it means a lot that, on the *same night* that he was betrayed, Jesus took the bread into his hands and, as he tore it, offered his own brokenness as a gift, a fellowship, a grace, to be shared by the helpless and broken in every generation.

Not all dying people participate in any sense in the Christian tradition, of course, and for others, it may help to find other means of expressing life's hidden grace, actions or images fundamental to all humanity. The lighting of a candle is one such universal image; also the gathering of condensed expressions of the natural world – a flower or growing plant, a pebble, aromatic oil, a little indoor fountain. Eating together can be very powerful too. Often a terminally ill person is separate from the fellowship of shared food; in hospice and hospital, sometimes the patient will eat one thing while visiting friends eat at the coffee shop, or from another menu. At home, special meals may be prepared for the one who is ill. But there is a power of solidarity and belonging in shared food. I have seen friends of a dying person bring in fish and chips or a bottle of wine to share around a bedside, and the sick person participate in the circle of love by taking a sip of wine through a straw, or nibbling at one or two chips.

Dying people may not need to eat, but they may desperately need to belong, to be loved, to be reassured that they have their place in humanity, right to the end.

In choosing symbols to help express spiritual reality, the

differences of faiths and denominations should be taken into account. For some, a little wooden cross to hold is a comfort, a lifeline to inner strength; to others it is an abhorrent thing: spiritual carers need to know which Christian denominations foster the understanding of the cross as a symbol of hope and comfort, and which disallow it as a taboo object. The same holds true of religious statues; for some the Virgin is an image of serenity and acceptance, for others such a statue is an ominous idol. For some a statue of the Buddha is a reminder of the grace and peace and strength of the inner self; for some fundamentalist Christians it would be a sign of occult practice and idolatry, evoking suspicion and distrust.

The power of sacrament and symbol lies in the spiritual concepts they evoke and embody; spiritual carers need to be knowledgeable about this, knowledgeable about the spiritual language of different faiths; and then sacrament and symbol can be used with great healing and strengthening power, as a particularly valuable aspect of spiritual power, especially where people do not easily articulate ideas in words, or are deeply rooted in a particular religious tradition.

### LOVING AND FAREWELLS

In giving spiritual care, one objective is the enhancing of a sense of meaning; enabling people to find, amid what for the most part feels chaotic, disintegrative and futile, dignity and peace.

As the time of death is perceived to be drawing near, there is often for dying people and their loved ones a tremendous release in the expression of meaning, truth and inner realities. So much so, that if the arrival of death does not then materialize, but the patient's condition ceases to deteriorate and reaches a plateau for a few days or weeks, there can be a feeling of redundancy, almost of embarrassment. The goodbyes, the 'I love you's have been said,' it is time to go.

One can observe this at other times in life: at summer-school conferences or parish weekends, occasions of short-lived closeness, often an emotional intensity is experienced between the participants which is peculiar to occasions when time is brief. Times of goodbye in particular are emotionally forgiving;

differences can be forgotten and reconciliation attained, on the understanding that separation is imminent. It is not unknown for a breakdown in relationship to follow when a partner diagnosed as terminally ill makes an unexpected recovery.

Perhaps human nature cannot stand too much scrutiny in such matters as this. Let it be enough that in spiritual care of the dying and their loved ones, the terminal phase, with its possibility of exchanges full of meaning and love, moments that can be cherished for ever, can be a healing and enriching period.

For this reason (and for others) it is helpful to keep the dying person and those close to him/her fully informed about the situation, to be truthful, and not try to hide the facts. If someone is dying, it is helpful to them to know what is happening. Sometimes it may need communicating gently and gradually, but they need to know. And in almost every case, they somehow know already; whether by instinct or by reading the non-verbal communications of those around them. Nobody should have snatched from them the chance to say goodbye, to resolve unfinished business, to leave the world in peace. The passage of dying is much eased by permitting these things to be addressed.

Spiritual carers have to learn the skill, not only of being good communicators, but of enabling others to communicate. A person responsible for spiritual care will sometimes have the task of breaking bad news of death or imminent death; sometimes the task of helping people stuck in habits of hostility, superficial defensive banter or avoidance of frightening subjects to learn to talk to each other, to learn to enter the scary territory of tears and touch and helplessness.

To be present, but not intrusive; to keep people company, but on their journey, not ours; to be authentically oneself, yet to know how to efface oneself: these are the necessary skills for spiritual care.

One of the loveliest compliments ever paid me was something said by a man in the last weeks of his life. I held his hand and said a prayer with him, and afterwards he took my hand in both of his and turned it over and looked at it. 'Ah,' he said, 'you could hold a bird in your hand.' Journeying with people in the time of their dying, the time of their loss, sometimes feels a little like taking a wild bird into the cradling cup of one's hands: such fragility, and such intense life; such a fine division between panic and trust; and such a rare privilege.

It is a gift of grace to find the strength needed to be, for people at such times, a mediator of God's gentleness.

# 5

# *The Lost Self*

Throughout life we define ourselves by our relationships, understanding and expressing our selves by conforming or not conforming to social norms; hungering for approval, affirmation and love; finding a flowering of identity in our experience of friendship, kinship, belonging to social and ideological groupings.

## Who am I?

Naomi's mother                                     An Orthodox Jew

Paul's partner

The rector of this parish                          Sally's uncle

John's wife

The man who empties your dustbins

Simon's godfather        The Chairman of the Bowls Club

The Medical Director of the Hospice

We define ourselves by labels that attach us to other people. In the experience of bereavement, as in the experience of dying, we lose our selves. One recently bereaved woman told me:

> I ask myself, 'How are you, Ann?' And in reply my soul shows itself to me. It has been torn, mutilated, by losing him. When I think of my soul now, I see something like a body, but a body from which half the face, one of the shoulders, part of the arms and the hands have been sheared away. Where they used to be are the flat surfaces of recent scar tissue. I – my soul – I am not whole without him. It is an amputee soul now. Time may 'heal' those wounds, but time will never give him back to me, or give me back my soul as it was.

Perhaps the most important aspect of grief work is that of exploring and discovering the new self, the new identity, and absorbing and adapting to the ways in which that identity changes over passing weeks and months.

The work of bereavement and grief belongs equally to the one who is dying and to the loved ones who share the journey and will be left behind. To experience dying is to experience the loss of the self, and to be bereaved is a kind of death; so that when we speak about bereavement, what is said applies also to a person who is dying, and what we say about one who is dying may also be said about one who is being bereaved. They stand together, and each experiences the rending of loss as their ways begin to part.

If it is true that we receive our identity to a great extent through relationship, then it follows that a dying or bereaved person's experience of their changing identity will be strongly influenced by the attitudes and regard of their spiritual carers – their companions on the journey.

The best way to help someone to find his or her identity is to listen, listen, listen: and to receive that gift of humanity with reverence, respect and love.

### THE NEED TO ADDRESS THE DEAD

For every spiritual carer keeping company with recently bereaved people, addressing the dead will sooner or later become something to consider. It is as well to have given it some thought before the need to act or speak in this area arises; for not only is it controversial, but it presents itself most urgently in those who are in deep and agonizing grief – those who cannot bear to be parted from the ones they have lost.

Most people fall into the category of those who believe that after death existence continues, and that in the afterlife the relationships of this life are in some manner renewed or continued. It takes little thought to realize that some very difficult questions arise out of this belief. Jesus himself met one such question. Somebody asked him about a widow, who according to tradition, had married one of her dead husband's six brothers. The brother then died and she married the next brother. As all the brothers were short-lived, by the time the woman died she had been married to all seven. The question asked was: 'Whose wife will the woman be on the day of resurrection?' Jesus said that you have to look at it differently; but we don't really understand.

We say that love is eternal, stronger than death, the power to defeat all other powers. Then we meet the questions: *How* does it outlive death? Will we be reunited? Can he still hear me . . . see me . . . speak to me? And what should we say?

For many bereaved people, the questions are interesting, but not urgent. The man who has been bereaved of a very elderly aunt, whom he held in affection but only occasionally visited during her years of dementia in the nursing home, may say she has gone to heaven and will be the first to greet him there with the offer of a cup of tea. But he is unlikely to lose much sleep over when that will be, or in what relationship he stands to her in the meantime.

There are others, though, for whom the questions burn and torment. Those who were body and soul entwined, those for whom bereavement is a rending apart of the fabric of being: who without the beloved are torn and wounded in their souls. There are some for whom life becomes a mocking exile, a separation made bearable only by the hope of seeing the loved one again. And they ask:

'Where is she?'
'He is here in this house – he *is* – isn't he?'
'I saw him in a dream, and he spoke to me – do you think I'm mad? It was so real.'

And what do we reply?

These questions and questioners are very often the ones that are passed on to the parish priest, or the chaplain of the hospice or nursing home. Many nursing staff feel themselves out of their depth when faced with these questions, and even confident and competent spiritual carers hesitate on the edge of this mysterious territory.

For the Christian minister, there are two normal and conventional responses: what might be described respectively as the religious approach and the psychological approach (I am talking here about the thinking that *underlies* the minister's pastoral practice). The religious approach usually takes the line that we will one day be reunited, but that is in God's gift, and we must wait patiently, enduring the separation and trusting God. For some ministers, of course, there is the added possibility that separation will be eternal if the deceased did not profess any religious belief. In any case, this approach is usually clear that the present separation, be it temporary or permanent, is absolute. Other religions approach the matter differently (with a diversity of differences) and the help of spiritualist churches is often sought by bereaved people who in other circumstances would have little use for spiritualist practice.

The psychological approach is probably the most common one among modern priests and chaplains. This approach takes the line that the need to address or contact the dead is a part of one of the commonest phases of grief: denial. These ministers would feel that it is of great importance to support the bereaved people gently through the phase of denial, helping them gradually to loosen the ties of longing, and to accept that the beloved is dead and will never now return. Such an approach seeks to discourage the bereaved person from believing that there may be any real substance in the sense of continued contact with the deceased person, or the sense of lingering presence. It is also true that many modern priests and chaplains hold a considerable variety of interpretations of the Christian belief in resurrection, and consequently vary in their understanding of what kind of afterlife we might hope for, if any. There is nothing like the consensus of thought among clergy on this matter that lay people, especially those who have quite a loose relationship with the Church, tend to assume.

I do not really understand why Christian ministers so often react with such negative instincts to the need of the bereaved to address the dead. There is an uneasiness, an automatic dismissal, in their reaction that does not have the ring of considered theological response. I see a lack of the pondering and listening that belong with taking people's stories seriously.

What follows represents my own hesitant thoughts on the matter: I have more questions than answers, but I have seen and heard enough to become dissatisfied with the conventional approaches.

There are some people who have unfinished business that torments them. They do not especially want to be reunited with the deceased, but do want to put matters right. For example, a daughter may be tortured by guilt and regret for having allowed a dominating elderly mother to spend her last days in a nursing home, refusing to bring her into the family home. The daughter may have made a wise and sensible decision, knowing the mother would devastate family relationships, knowing that the mother–daughter relationship was not able to withstand the stresses of the demands of twenty-four-hour nursing. Even so, guilt is eating away at her, and she longs for the reassurance that her mother has forgiven her, longs to reassure her mother that she was loved.

If such a daughter came to seek my help, my response would vary according to my assessment of the individual, but would not exclude the possibility of asking or permitting the daughter to address the deceased mother, to pour out to her the guilt and the love and the sadness. I have seen remarkable peace and release obtained that way.

Many Christian ministers see such a scenario as an acceptable counselling technique, as no more than a means of enabling a bereaved daughter to get in touch with and express her painful emotions, to resolve her unfinished business.

More tentatively, I offer my thoughts about those who believe in the continued presence of the deceased, and continuing contact with the deceased.

It seems to me that neither the religious approach that maintains there is an absolute separation by death until (or beyond) the day of judgement nor the psychological approach that considers all sense of the deceased beloved's presence to be a form of denial takes sufficient account of the stories of bereaved people's actual experience: in this whole area we have been remarkably quick to say how it is, and remarkably slow to listen. That in itself should alert us to our own uneasiness, with its attendant danger of distorted judgement.

I have now met and listened to many intelligent, thoughtful, not at all fanciful people, people who know themselves well and who are not given to self-delusion, who genuinely and unshakeably believe that their deceased friend or relative has been in contact with them since death. For some, it has been only a momentary thing; like the woman who, on returning home from her father's funeral, had a sudden, unexpected and unsought, overwhelming sense of his presence, and that he wanted to tell her that all was well, he was all right: that and no more. For others it is an ongoing thing, sometimes a strange series of coincidences and dreams as well as a powerful sense of the beloved's presence.

It is easy, and it appears rational and grown-up, to dismiss these things as denial or superstition. But I think they are not. I cannot pretend to have any systematic thought about the way in which we relate once separated by death, but enough has happened in my journeying alongside bereaved people to convince me that it is not just simple: we are separated by a veil, a mist, a river – not by a wall or a steel barrier.

For dying people too, there are often experiences of being met, welcomed, as they approach the moment of death, by loved friends and family members who had previously died (sometimes even when the dying one had not known them to have died). These 'seeings', as well as the experience of being met by angels or other beings of spiritual significance, are not uncommon experiences. They are often dismissed as hallucinations, or wishful thinking, or as a product of the dying person's unconscious mind on sensing impending death. Of course we do well to listen with cautious wisdom: gullibility does not serve us well. But sceptical though we may feel, we *should* listen: we need all the spiritual education we can get.

I do have one very strong reservation in this area, however: that one should be wary, and encourage others to be wary, about seeking spiritual contact in the form of seances or other forms of groping into the spirit world. To open the doors of one's soul to unidentified incomers is not a wise proceeding, and is different from appreciating the dreams and odd occurrences that hint at the continuing company of the beloved.

## STAGES AND CYCLES OF GRIEF

Loss is a process more than an event or a state. There is nothing static about it. The experience of loss when someone is dying is also open at both ends, from the present into the past and from the present into the future. Someone who watches at the bedside of a dying partner experiences not only present pain, but relives the emotions of old griefs, and looks towards bleak months and years stretching ahead. Grief is on the one hand something which varies enormously across a range of different individuals, and on the other hand has some almost universal characteristics (this is recognized in the words the spiritual carer will often hear, 'You can only understand when you've been through it yourself').

Grief is necessarily cyclical. Humanity cannot bear unremitting pain. We switch off, buffer ourselves, look at the horror for a while, then look away, put our affairs in order, then talk as if we were going skiing in the spring.

The conversation of bereaved people can be disconcertingly cyclical, oscillating between relaxed chatting and quips about their new situation and the bits and pieces of everyday life to trembling disclosures of raw and bloody agony and lacerating emotional pain.

The time immediately following bereavement is often padded with a protective fog of shock. Numbness frequently dulls the pain of loss, and the legal and religious duties following a death fill up the time.

The pain of grief manifests itself differently in different people, but usually after the initial shock abates there is a period of deep grief, sometimes felt especially about six weeks after the bereavement, when the wound is still so raw, and yet the pain seems to have been going on for a long time. Then after that, the bereaved person may adjust, get 'back on their feet', and have interludes of feeling a little better, of 'coping', interspersed with sharp, unexpected, agonizing spells of grief. Anniversaries, special times and places, things and occurrences of shared significance with the loved one trigger episodes of grief pain.

It is remarkable how much variety there is in people's expectations of themselves. One will say, 'It's been a whole week now – I shouldn't still be behaving like this,' whereas another will describe the first anniversary of the death as 'early days yet'.

The five stages of grief which Elisabeth Kübler-Ross identified in her pioneering work among dying people form the foundation of our modern understanding of the grieving process. They are:

Denial   Anger   Bargaining   Depression   Acceptance

In calling them 'stages of grief', though, it is important to avoid any sense that they follow a particular order, or that all people experience all of them, or that once experienced they cannot recur. Rather than stages, it might be better to describe them as five aspects of grief, and to depict them in the form of a circle rather than a line:

These stages of grief are now basic to teaching on caring for grieving and dying people, and there are many texts which discuss them. Here I will add only a few observations of my own, since to do more would merely be to repeat what has been adequately dealt with elsewhere.

In the environment of the hospice where I have been a Free Church Chaplain, I have wondered if we are in some way sending out discouraging signals to people who are angry, because it surprises me how few people express a significant level of anger. Certainly it is very hard even for an informed and understanding carer to refrain from taking someone's anger personally. When the one you have tried to help, to soothe, to make comfortable is just furious; when your patient turns into an impatient, and nothing is right and all your decisions are met with suspicion, it takes a wise person to remember that anger is a stage of grief and there is no need to feel inadequate, a failure or afraid.

We have a tendency to back away from angry people, to be wary. This often fuels the fire of their suspicion, because fear very often communicates as shiftiness.

I have heard some therapists and counsellors speak of anger as a root or underlying emotion:

'She needs to get in touch with her anger.'
'He has a lot of anger to come out.'

For myself, I am more comfortable with the understanding of anger as a *masking* emotion – protecting a wound of sadness, fear, uncertainty or grief. Perhaps it is easier for me to see things that way as a carer: the reflection that 'He has a lot of anger to come out' may feel rather alarming, like caring for a simmering volcano. Seeing the anger and wondering what is the pain it conceals is less unnerving, and less personally threatening: perhaps I can help; feel my way past the anger to the wound it protects, maybe bring some healing there. Sometimes sick people get angry just because they are tired: there is no energy left to meet the tasks or expectations that confront them. Anger can be the only way to gain access to a burst of adrenalin that will release the needed energy.

For carers who feel nervous of an angry patient, it is worth remembering that sick and weary people find it very difficult to wait. It may be that the carer is trying to unearth deep psychological disturbance when the patient is simply being asked to wait too often, too long, and is humiliated by the helplessness and frustration of it, is made to feel like a child by the tears of exhaustion that are dangerously near the surface, is frightened of dirtying the bed, or of falling.

Denial is something I am often asked about. Carers sometimes feel at a loss to know how to react to someone who outlines ambitious plans for a grand party or a summer holiday when they are bedbound and terminally ill in hospital. The right response is a delicate balance. A patient is not helped by the carer going along with the denial – fetching brochures from the travel agent or party invitations from the stationer. On the other hand, the denial is needed for a moment as a buffer in the struggle to come to terms with the prospect of dying. The middle path seems to be best, that neither confirms the denial, nor rips away the protection it offers. So maybe when the man whose legs are paralysed by an encroaching and aggressively growing tumour says he is going skiing in Switzerland next spring, it might be most helpful to say, 'You must have really enjoyed your skiing holidays in Switzerland,' which neither confirms nor denies his hopes for the future, but leaves him an opening to talk about the pain of all he will be losing and leaving.

It might seem that acceptance is the perfect state, but it can be a bit unnerving for carers. Sometimes acceptance manifests as peace, tranquillity, but sometimes as a kind of remoteness. The patient can seem unreachable, inaccessible, beyond the needs to relate and engage that belong to this life. The carers' own needs for relationship can feel uncomfortably redundant in the presence of acceptance of death, when the patient's soul is resting quietly, waiting, the eyes of the spirit looking beyond the here and now.

My own experience of people in the bargaining phase of grief has been that it is something that requires me to do little more than listen and be there. It has felt to me like a very busy thing, an almost feverish activity of the soul. The energies of the person have seemed directed inwards, negotiating with God, questioning, coming to terms. Although it can be quite intense and painful, I have felt it as less demanding of myself as a carer than other aspects of grief.

As with anger, depression can be difficult for the carer keeping company with the one who is depressed. We long to make everything better, to take away the pain. There can be few things that teach us to live with our own helplessness more effectively than someone else's depression.

It would be a mistake to assume that what begins in denial must conclude in acceptance, with anger, bargaining and depression as the intervening modes. Such an assumption predisposes a carer to feel a failure when a patient dies angry, or bargaining, or in denial, not 'accomplishing' the acceptance they 'should' have 'achieved'. These are observed aspects of grief, not stages in the syllabus of 'A'-level suffering. They are for recognizing and understanding, and there is no 'ought to' about moving on.

STILLBIRTH, MISCARRIAGE AND TERMINATION OF PREGNANCY

Though better understood by some than in previous years, there is still considerable variation in the sensitivity with which the person bereaved by stillbirth or miscarriage is met.

Many hospitals now appreciate the need for the parents of a stillborn child to have a proper rite of passage in laying the child to rest, and for there to be mementoes of the short life, such as a photograph. Indeed, there may be a need for the hospital chaplain to take particular care in allowing the meaning and value of the lost baby to be expressed in the funeral service, and to affirm that although the child's life was so brief, it had all the holiness and precious significance of every human life.

Candles, flowers, lovely clothes to dress the baby in; everything should be considered and offered in order to communicate to the bereaved parents (and maybe grandparents too) that their loss and pain have been seen and heard, and their child's life is worthy of respect and love.

For those who have lost a baby through miscarriage, especially early miscarriage, there may be the pain of bereavement without the help of a body to bury. Sometimes those early babies go the way of the lavatory or the sluice, or cannot be found among the products of the womb when the miscarriage occurs. It often happens too that bereavement through miscarriage, termination or stillbirth remains a secret grief carried through the years. Sooner or later such grief will surface, and must be acknowledged and responded to properly so that the bereaved person can find again a possibility of peace and wholeness, so that the hidden wound be touched and permitted to heal. In this circumstance, as well as listening to the bereaved person's story, it may help to offer a retrospective service of remembrance and thanksgiving for the lost child, a chance for the pain of loving and regret to come out.

Those who lose babies may also be losing their identity as a parent, or losing their sense of themselves as an adequate parent. They may be losing their sense of the world as a safe and nurturing place. They may have lost their comfortable place among their circle of friends and family (especially among other parents of babies, or circles such as the clinic ante-natal class or National Childbirth Trust class groups). The loss of self-in-relation should be taken seriously, even though the relationship was a short one.

In bereaved people who have lost a baby through termination of pregnancy, there is also the possibility that the decision to terminate the pregnancy will have been influenced by family and friends. If this is so, there may be a multiple loss to face: the loss of self-esteem through not being strong enough to withstand the pressure of other people's opinions; bereavement through loss of trust in family and friends; the loss of the child; the loss of the self as a mother; the loss of someone of one's own. The decision to terminate a pregnancy may have to be made quickly and under pressure. When the decision is prompted by reasons other than urgent medical necessity, it may imply a belief that this world is a place with not enough space, not enough generosity, to welcome everyone. The implications of such a belief for the one who makes the decision are enormous. The spiritual carer who has the opportunity to accompany people in this situation through their grieving may need to help them find a vision of a world made by the love of God, in which everyone has a place and is wanted.

### FINDING AND ACCEPTING IDENTITY

I remember seeing Christiaan Barnard interviewed on television in the early days of heart transplant operations. His interviewer asked him the name of the donor for that first successful operation, and Barnard did not know. Surprised, the interviewer persisted with his questioning: 'You don't know the donor's *name?*' But Barnard shrugged: 'It was just a corpse.'

In those words are encapsulated an insensitivity and ignorance about the spiritual needs of bereaved people that is so monumental it takes my breath away.

Before anything else, spiritual care is about *identity.* Prayer, religion, philosophy, sacraments – all may play their part, but first and foremost spiritual care is about identity.

Spirituality is all about who one is, and that is found only in relationship: with other people, the ones who make up our world, and with that foundational reality that believers call God.

For proper spiritual care to be given, there must be an affirmation of the dying or bereaved person's identity as a unique individual, as someone who matters: not as the grist to the hospital's mill, or as the consumer of the National Health product, or even as the grateful and admiring recipient of the wonderful ethos of the hospice, but as a spiritual free self, a being of dignity and worth. It is important that those who select and appoint spiritual carers look for people who regard others in that way, who will hear and see and never patronize. I am not sure that this quality in a spiritual carer can be taught: perhaps it is an awakening, a realization, able to be recognized but not communicated. It is an attitude that one could pick up maybe, but not a lesson that one could apply. Techniques of care and listening can be taught, but not that fundamental vision of the spirituality of human encounter.

Terminal illness mounts a serious attack on the sense of identity. The powerlessness, loneliness and fear commonly experienced feel dehumanizing and alienating, and constitute (or trigger) spiritual crisis in many people.

It is hard to believe in a God who cares, who is merciful and offers security, in a life situation where all that was reliable and familiar is disintegrating; where one's own territory is lost and the new environment is not home.

It is virtually impossible to maintain spiritual equilib-rium when one's own being is coming apart; when physical functioning is haywire, mental processes are embarrassingly unpredictable, and emotions are ricocheting all over the place in the desperate attempt to adjust, to assimilate, and to maintain the dignity of appearing normal.

The sense of self is enhanced by creating an environment for self to live: my choice of clothes, whether I live in a flat or a house, the fabrics and carpeting and furniture I have chosen, my ornaments and pictures and crockery, whether I eat supper at the table or curled up on the sofa with a tray on my lap, whether I decorate my home with tree and lights and tinsel at Christmas or put candles on the table for a dinner party, if I keep a cat as a companion – all of this is how I offer my identity to the world, and arrive at a sense of self.

Sometimes, I find it embarrassingly difficult to locate a friend in a hospital ward. Night-clothes, unlike day clothes, tend to have a general pale similarity. It is only by looking at the face in each bed that I can find my friend.

People in terminal illness often have to face the decision to sell their home. They have to find a new home for loved pet animals. In hospital they may be encouraged to wear night-clothes. The choice of how or when or what to eat is limited by the possibilities of institutional provision. No more candles on the dinner table; no longer my plates, my wallpaper, my sofa. People who appreciate enormously the care and love they are given still sit in the beds of caring institutions, saying with tears in their eyes, 'It's so hard to give up my home.'

Those with the strongest, most insistent sense of identity sometimes insist on going home, on staying there until every possibility of managing has been exhausted.

I had a schoolfriend who used to say, 'I want to go home: not where I live, but home.' Good spiritual care understands that it is not things, but the self that has been lost to a terminally ill person coming into institutional care. Like a dance or a song or a painting, the environment of home was the person's song of creation in the world: to lose it is to lose one's own space, to live in the world as a refugee.

This sense of self being lost is echoed in the responses of others. It is easy for institutional staff to treat patients as though they had no spiritual presence, and hard to know quite who they are if they cannot speak or hear properly, and have nothing of their own round about the room to indicate the contours of their personality. I have been interested to notice how much easier it is for staff to relate as a person with someone who has brought pictures and little things from home into the institution. Likewise, patients who wear clothes, not nighties or pyjamas, seem to attract a better understanding of their individuality.

An aspect of individuality which must be respected and celebrated by spiritual carers is that of sexuality. Often people cease to be regarded as sexual beings once they come into an institution to be cared for. However, there is more to sexuality than sexual activity, and sexuality is an essential element of identity and personality whether or not a person is sexually active.

Difficulty with this can arise in two main areas. A person who is confused or suffering from dementia may say or do things which are sexually inappropriate, and this can be experienced as disturbing or threatening by nursing staff. The nurses must have confidential space and time to express their own feelings and concerns about this, and some suitable approach to the situation has to be found, otherwise an attitude of hostility and fear may develop towards the patient.

A further area of difficulty may arise when nursing staff are uncomfortable with a patient's sexual orientation. It is good for nursing staff and members of the spiritual care team to have space to talk through their feelings about being a companion on the journey of someone who has a sexual orientation different from their own. These matters are right at the core of a person's sense of self and identity, and to ask dying and bereaved people to accommodate prejudice and hostility in their carers is to ask too much. It is also discourteous, cruel, and bad practice.

Spiritual care involves nurturing again the bruised and diminished sense of self. In order for this to happen, not only the patients, but also the carers must bring the stamp of their own personality to bear on the situation, being self-expressive and self-giving without being self-indulgent. In an institution where one has responsibility in the area of spiritual care, it is important to recognize that another person may relate better than oneself to a particular patient. Here lies the value for spiritual care of chaplaincy/nursing teamwork.

For spiritual carers working within institutions, it is very important to listen carefully and look carefully, making eye contact, addressing the patients directly, making sure they know they have been really seen and really heard. If a person has expressed distress and frustration at the status of 'patient', this should be acknowledged and not belittled. The person's individuality and identity should be affirmed by the spiritual carer in creating a sense of not rushing and a sense of private space (see Ch. 2), in loving and respectful body language, maybe using touch. Any religious or ideological concerns of the patient should be recognized and maybe mentioned. Above all else, till the last breath, this is a person with a name, a shining light of selfhood, dust of Adam, of Eve, brought into life by the breath of the living God.

# 6

# *Mainly about Funerals*

In this chapter there is a lot of talk about clergy and ordained ministers. This is because most funerals are taken by ordained people. However, anybody can take a funeral, just as anybody can offer spiritual care; what is true for clergy here applies to lay people also.

## FUNERALS AND SERVICES OF REMEMBRANCE

The funeral is a milestone in the process of grieving. Very often bereaved people will refer to it as a point of change:

'I'll be all right when the funeral's over.'
'I'm just waiting for the funeral, really.'
'I won't really feel we've laid him to rest until the funeral.'

It is usually one of the most significant moments of farewell, and often marks the earliest point of moving on, the pivot of the aftermath of death and life as it will be. In saying this, I want to be absolutely clear that no one should expect that after a funeral the days of grieving are concluded. On the contrary, the funeral may be the trigger for real grieving to begin after the original numbing of shock.

For some the funeral is emotionally harrowing, an event of felt significance. For others it is a ritual of decency and respect undertaken without emotion. It is important for spiritual carers to understand, though, that whatever perceptions people have of the funeral, there is a deep, universal human need for a rite of passage to mark the death.

Bereaved people may say that the funeral meant nothing to them (at the time anyway), but it is certain that the absence of a funeral (for example, when the person who died has expressed a wish that there be no funeral, or when an unborn baby dies) hinders bereaved people from moving on, leaves unfinished business, adds to the trauma of grief.

## The Spiritual Care of Dying and Bereaved People

Because this rite of passage is so important, there is usually a sense that it must be done 'properly'. Ordained clergy are often asked to conduct funerals of people they do not know and who have no particular religious conviction, not out of a fear of God, but because the clergy are official representatives of spirituality, and their presence places a stamp of formality which feels appropriate at such a significant time.

However, a note of confusion can arise here, especially in our culture which is in the main a post-Christian, secular culture.

Christian ministers sometimes perceive a funeral as an opportunity to preach the gospel. Presented with a captive audience who never normally go to church, this can seem like a God-given chance to present the Christian beliefs regarding death, resurrection and faith in Jesus Christ.

If the person who has died was a staunch believer, then the teaching of the Church may have a proper place in the funeral address: but I do not believe that to be especially helpful where the one who has died was not a religious person.

A funeral can be regarded as principally either an act of worship, or as a rite of passage. If it is seen *principally* as an act of worship, then religious faith will feature prominently in the wording of the ceremony and the address. The occasion still functions as a rite of passage, of course. If the funeral is seen principally as a rite of passage, then its religious content can vary considerably, reflecting the life philosophy of the mourners and the deceased.

The difficulty arises when the minister perceives the occasion as principally an act of worship, but the mourners perceive it as a rite of passage. Then the words of the ceremony will be very Christian, expressing sometimes quite complicated theology in not very accessible language, and the address will be about Jesus who is risen more than about John who has died. Particularly if the minister makes little mention of the deceased person's name, the mourners can be left with a vague feeling of disappointment; their moment of loving tribute, the solemnity of farewell, will have been diminished.

Most people hold a belief in God, but neither clearly nor strongly. When they come to a funeral, they are looking inwards, and properly so. It is a time of memories, a time of coming to terms with loss, a time of sadness and tears. It is not

70

a time for listening intently to complex Pauline exposition of resurrection theology, nor is it a time to require people to start considering doctrine.

When the funeral is a religious ceremony other than Christian – Muslim or Hindu, for example – or when the Christian flavour is very specific – for example, Greek Orthodox or Strict Brethren (a branch of the Plymouth Brethren) – then the act of worship and the rite of passage function as one seamless thing. It is that majority of funerals, where the deceased is 'C of E-ish' or 'not really religious, but her brother is' or 'used to go to the Methodist Chapel years back, but hasn't been since his wife died', where sensitivity is needed to conduct a ceremony which will offer spiritual comfort and support in a way that feels relevant and appropriate.

If there were to be only two golden rules for funerals, they would have to be:

- Get the name of the deceased right, and use it.
- Get in touch with the mourners before the funeral, and make a house call if possible.

Basic? It is surprising how often even these two simple things are neglected. Whatever may happen on the day – if the organ breaks down, or you leave the notes for your address at home, or the mourners of the next funeral gather noisily outside the chapel door – if these two simple things have been done, the mourners will feel that you cared. If they are neglected, no amount of pomp and ceremony will give to the occasion the right sense of spiritual comfort and properly expressed farewell.

It is the achieving of this sense of being cared for – loving the people – which really preaches the gospel at a funeral. Mourners know and recognize the religious status of a Christian minister. They understand this to be a representative of God, of religious faith; there is no need to hammer it home. There is no need for a minister to go home feeling uneasy after a funeral which contained no mention of Jesus Christ. I learned something of this from taking the funeral of an avowed atheist with an atheist family. They had requested prayers in case any friends or relatives harboured unsuspected religious faith: but the more I considered it, the more inappropriate this seemed.

In the end, we had a ceremony with no prayers, no Bible readings, and a blessing which did not refer specifically to God. In the address, which was a tribute to the life of the deceased, I spoke briefly about my own faith – faith in a God who does not take umbrage at our failure to notice the presence of grace. I was intrigued to learn, after this spiritual but non-religious ceremony, of someone who had been inspired by the occasion, saying it had made her feel almost like going to church again. Sometimes the gospel is better preached by silence. You can have the gospel without religion; you cannot have the gospel without love.

Because the funeral is a rite of passage – a human ceremony with deeper and more ancient roots than the Christian faith – a memorial service and ritual observance of the death are still needed by mourners who have no religious faith. These usually have a Christian form and shape because of the Christian background of our culture. It is tradition which gives force and weight to the ceremony of the occasion. If mourners were happy to say a few words of their own, and make their farewells without the help of a clergy person they do not know, they could do so. But the clergy are wanted for the weight of the spiritual tradition behind them, to bless the departing soul with peace.

The house call which precedes the funeral can be a very therapeutic time for the mourners, and should not be rushed. It is a time to tell the story, to air regrets and anxieties, to turn over the treasures of memory. If the one conducting the funeral has a notebook and a sharp ear for a turn of phrase, the words of the address can be flavoured with the vocabulary of the mourners and remembered words of the deceased. This gives to those at the funeral a sense of having been really heard and understood. It is an important thing, that funeral address. The atmosphere in the chapel can change dramatically from one of people wrapped in their own thoughts during the opening prayers and readings, to almost unnervingly acute attention as the address begins.

Not only the address but the prayers can reflect the character of the person who has died, and the particular overtones of loss which colour this individual bereavement. It may be a rending agony, a death for which the mourners were not ready, maybe leaving a feeling of guilt and shame. Or it may be the peaceful conclusion of a long and fulfilled life: or the sudden death of a child. It makes no sense to use the same form of words for every death. This is the occasion when words, which seem so futile and empty in much of the journey alongside dying and bereaved people, have their moment. This is the time to explore the colour and flavour and texture of words, to find the right ones to weave the shroud for this precious soul, beloved of God, embarking on the momentous journey.

Again, the wording should carefully respect the outlook of the mourners and the deceased. I have spoken about the soul embarking on a journey; but for materialist atheists, life ends with the dying of the body, and an essential part of the grieving is the harshness of that fact. Then can be the time to speak about the power of memory; for our memories make us what we are. In that sense, if in no other, the deceased is part of eternity, part of the enduring fabric of humanity.

## WHEN THE MOURNERS DID NOT LOVE THE DECEASED

The simple and usual pattern of the grief of bereavement is when the bereaved people loved and miss the one who has died. The grief is for the loss of that beloved one, all they meant, grief that this separation is final, as far as this world goes.

There are deaths we mourn only a little. The death of relatives we never knew closely – the old lady whom we knew as 'auntie', but always seemed remote. The death of a member of a group or community we belong to; church, the bowls club, the Women's Institute, a colleague from work. Sometimes the death of a public figure, someone we never knew personally, but whose work we admired: or the death of a tutor or employer, someone known, but not intimately.

Deaths such as these are true bereavements, and sometimes, especially if a series of such bereavements occurs, can leave us a legacy of grief we do not acknowledge or even really recognize. The relationship during life may not seem, rationally, to warrant the sense of loss we feel. If our response is one of denial, telling ourselves not to be silly and self-indulgent, refusing ourselves time to explore and live through the bereavement, we may store up trouble for later. Very often a bereavement powerfully triggers previous, unacknowledged emotions of

73

grief, revealing a compound of loss. Sometimes loss is deliberately buried by other concerns. A marriage dies, and the pain is concealed by working hard at a career. A parent falls ill and personal grief is set aside for the practicalities of caring. The parent dies and there are other relatives to be helped through their grief. One's own grief is turned from again in catching up lost time at work. The dog dies, and that is rejected as too trivial to be a matter for serious grief. Then one day in the cinema, watching the drama of a man suffering terminal illness and death, tears out of all proportion come flooding out, and the dam gives way.

We should be gentle with others, and gentle with ourselves. We should also give ourselves space for tears. As spiritual carers accompanying others on their journey, we take the rôle of supporter. When the one we are accompanying dies, and our rôle finishes, it is not over-emotional, does not signify over-involvement, if we weep at that loss. The best spiritual carers love. There is no love that knows loss without pain.

There is another kind of loss, a difficult, painful grief, which occurs when a person is bereaved of someone they were close to, but did not love. This might be the dutiful daughter of a selfish and demanding parent, or the homophobic brother of a gay man. It is not so bad when the bereaved person is the one who initiated the estrangement (as in the second example), although negativity in a chief mourner towards the deceased person's lifestyle can severely hamper the appropriate expressions of mourning in the funeral arrangements for the deceased's other loved ones.

The really sharp pain comes when, after struggling ineffectually to improve a difficult relationship, a bereaved person is left rejected right to the end. When the deceased has persisted to death with rejection and estrangement, the bereaved person suffers a multiple loss:

> the loss of the one who has died;
> the loss of hope that reconciliation might yet be achieved;
> the loss of the sense of a right to grieve.

When a person dies, an extraordinary thing happens, in the spiritual dimension: it is as though a puff of energy – like the ink trail of a squid, the wake of a ship, the smoke, dust and flame of a rocket launch – is released into the lives of those who had a spiritual connection with the deceased person. That puff of energy works with a transformative power consistent with the flavour and character of the person who has died. One can learn something about the person who has died by watching and waiting afterwards. Love, unexpected friendships and hope and possibility are released like a sweet fragrance in the wake of some lives.

A very clear example of the wake a death leaves is seen in the lives of those who have lost a loved one by suicide. The unsustainable wound of living which made death seem the obvious, only choice, spreads on death to those who are left behind. The legacy of futility, guilt and sorrow that a suicide leaves is a terrible price for partners, children and parents to pay. The unhealable wound does not close at death; it transfers its pain to those left behind who were dearest and closest.

Those who to the end of their lives continue in determined hatred and selfishness leave a wake of bitterness and acrid grief. The funeral services of such people are painful. The grief of having lost for ever the hope of reconciliation is hard to heal. When a rejecting parent dies, the bereaved child loses both the actual parent and the hoped-for, dreamed-of parent. It is the grief of seeing a dream cherished against all rational hope finally shatter. The look on the faces of such people moves me very much. They do not often weep, because the natural release of mourning death has been denied them by the withholding of the relationship in life.

There are also some who fulfilled their obligations as a close relative or partner, but long since ceased to love the deceased, if they ever loved them in the first place. The funeral is one last obligation – 'Well, we gave him a decent burial.'

Preparing a funeral and a funeral address in such circumstances as these is a time of much gnawing the pencil end or staring helplessly at the blank word-processor screen. 'What can I say?' one thinks desperately. 'There is nothing to say.'

That experience of nothingness, of futility and hopelessness, is itself an important part of the companionship on the journey of the one so painfully bereaved. But healing words, words that are gentle and bring hope, must be found. However much or little religion characterizes the funeral, it will have the touch of Christ if it brings healing and hope.

In these circumstances, the bereaved person may express a sense of futility about the funeral service, perhaps remarking that there is little point in an address where there is nothing good to say. But the need for a proper expression of mourning is in fact extremely important for a person bereaved in this way: in some ways far more important than for a person bereaved of a relationship of mutual love and trust. In fact, it is often the case that where the relationship between the bereaved and the deceased was fragile or remote, the bereaved can become very possessive about the funeral arrangements, excluding other mourners. It is their last chance to assert the relationship. Those mourners who are sure of the love of the one who has died are often very generous in their attitudes, content to take a back seat on the day of the funeral.

In some funerals it is possible to observe a distinct contrast between the relaxed and unobtrusive behaviour of the ones who know the deceased loved them, and the determined self-assertion of those tied by blood or duty, but not by love.

In all of these circumstances, it is the task of the officiant at the ceremony to sense the atmosphere, assess the situation, and conduct the ceremony so as to leave the way open to healing and friendship, and give comfort and reassurance to every mourner. The Christian religion offers those who conduct funerals the marvellous advantage of being able to state with confidence, of even those who were heartily loathed by everyone, that we commend them to the mercy of the God who is love, in whose eyes they were always precious.


## HOMOSEXUALITY AND DEATH

Week by week church attenders are in a minority. Most people do not come to church every single Sunday, yet most of those who do not come have a sense of the numinous, a religious instinct which prompts them to come to church to mark life events of significance – and maybe at Christmas, which has become an annual event of human significance as well as a religious (Christian and pre-Christian) feast.

For heterosexual people, the life events to be celebrated in church are usually three: their wedding(s), the baptisms of their children, and funerals. Two joyful occasions, one sorrowful. Weddings, baptisms and funerals are times of family get-togethers, reinforcing bonds of affection and belonging.

Some gay men and lesbians have children of course; some have been, or are, married; some are baptised as adults. However, in the main, it is true that weddings and baptisms are not life events for the gay community as they are for the straight. It is *infant* baptism which is the rite of passage ceremony sought by those whose belief is hazy, not adult baptism; and infant baptism belongs with heterosexuality in the vast majority of cases.

This means that gay men and lesbians are left with funerals for their only significant ceremony. I have realized in taking funerals for gay men that they were saying to each other 'We only seem to meet at funerals these days', where straight people were saying 'We only meet up at weddings (baptisms) and funerals'. Gay men and lesbians do not have the two joyful life events – only the sorrowful one.

AIDS has compounded this for gay men: in that both the prevalence of AIDS infection among gay men, in this country, and the tremendous work done by gay men to turn the tide of public and institutional attitudes towards those living with AIDS, have made AIDS awareness and AIDS memorial events a significant feature and focus of the gay community in our society. Another link with death.

The Church still carries much homophobia and rejection of gay men and lesbians, although attitudes are gentler now than twenty years ago. Part of the increase in gentleness is expressed in that the Church will relent towards gay men when they die, though it will not affirm them in their life. This means that funerals in which gay orientation and partnership are now acknowledged can take place, and so can AIDS services. For example, in World AIDS Week there are often church events, brave and heart-wrenching celebrations of life.

### THE ROAD TO EMMAUS

The Bible tells many stories of people meeting with God in the course of a journey. Two of the great journey stories of the New Testament are the story of Saul's vision of Christ on the road to Damascus (told in Acts 9.1–9), and the story of the resurrection appearance of Jesus on the road to Emmaus (told in Luke 24.13–32). The story of the road to Damascus is dramatic and powerful: a blinding flash, bright enough to blind, a dramatic revelation, a sudden and instantaneous conversion. It is an archetype of the way some people meet with God.

The story of the road to Emmaus is different. Two friends travelling together, on foot, trying to make sense of their bereavement and all that had happened to them. An anonymous third person joins them, and, walking along with him, they find he brings them insight where before they had only confusion. Arriving at their destination, they turn to the stranger with an invitation: 'Stay with us now, for night is falling . . .' The stranger stays, and is their guest for the evening meal. He takes the bread in his hands and breaks it, and, in that familiar gesture, they know him for the Christ, the holy one. For most people, grace is an unrecognized and unacknowledged presence, bringing to the companions on the journey insight, meaning, peace.

On the road to Damascus, the prayer is of a visionary, religious nature:

'Who are you, Lord?'

'I am Jesus . . .'

But the prayer on the road to Emmaus, 'Stay with us now, for night is falling,' is not religious, does not recognize the Christ; only recognizes the ordinary human value of the shared journey, the shared meal, hospitality at nightfall.

Both the road to Damascus and the road to Emmaus are valid archetypes of religious experience. Sudden or gradual, a thing of mystical vision or of ordinary human relationship, grace may explode or slant gently into our lives. When Christ comes to us, some of us fall down and worship him, others chat along with him all unawares, and invite him in to tea. And some never tell the story, because they do not realize who it is they have met. In those untold stories of unrecognized grace, I have no doubt that the Christ came: he comes to everyone. And I think it does not matter that he was not known for himself. The beauty of Jesus is not in the eye of the beholder, but in the kindness of God.

## DEATHBED CONVERSION, HELLFIRE, AND EVANGELISTIC ZEAL

Christianity is a faith which believes in conversion; a missionary faith; a faith of saving souls; an evangelistic faith.

Yet one can believe all this and still be happy to do no proselytizing at all.

Traditionally, the saving of a soul has been seen in terms of persuading someone to acquiesce to Christian doctrine. Any means have been seen as valid means to this end: torture and force, as in the days of the Spanish Inquisition; guile and deception, as in today's Friendship Evangelism, in which the establishing of a relationship is a grooming process for conversion; intellectual argument and apologetics; and the time-honoured use of psychological terror, playing upon the fear of death, alienation and abandonment that finds a corner in most human hearts.

'Giving your heart to Jesus', or being received into the Church, or undergoing baptism – whatever a particular Christian grouping sees as the decisive step – an emphasis is placed on conscious assent as the activating factor for the salvation of the soul. 'Soul' and 'intellect' and 'conscious mind' and 'will' are entwined concepts in our culture. This is reflected in the Church's emphasis on study and intellectual ability in spiritual development and selection for spiritual leadership. For the Church, the central authority has tended to be 'The Word', 'The Book', and God is 'The Lord', 'Almighty God', a somewhat inflexible, highly demanding patriarchal figure: 'a jealous God'. Watch your p's and q's with *him*!

Coming from that context, especially when such a theological outlook has been swallowed unquestioningly, journeying with dying people can be a challenging thing for a Christian minister. Sometimes Christian ministers come to hospice work expecting to be on the lookout for opportunities for discreet proselytizing: a chance to 'talk about the Lord'.

There can be dislocation of understanding between chaplaincy staff and nursing staff in palliative care. An agnostic or atheist nurse may see the adopting of religious faith in a dying patient as pathological, a form of denial; while the chaplaincy staff may see it as an acceptance of reality, an emergence into clearer spiritual light. Certainly red-hot religion in dying patients and their relatives can be bewildering and repellent to those who have to nurse them (especially if they find themselves the object of the patient's last evangelistic efforts!), and is often interpreted as a cover for acute fear of death. It may be; it is a cover for fear of life often enough.

Most hospice and hospital chaplains are very cautious about the spiritual carers they let loose on their patients; evangelistic zeal is an automatic barrier to working with people who are dying. Coercive persuasion to particular philosophies or outlooks is not regarded as helpful.

But we should examine the theological questions that stir around this issue, because they remain under the surface as a cause of uneasiness; there are many hospice chaplains whose theology is at variance with their pastoral practice, and many whose pastoral experience has reshaped their theology completely.

The questions are about what kind of God is God (see also Ch. 1), heaven and hell, salvation and damnation, conditional or unconditional love, trust and fear.

Something that hampers us enormously in spiritual ministry is when our idea of God is as a commodity rather than as a person. (Some theologians are adamant that God is personal but not a person, but I don't want to split hairs like that here.)

When we see God like that, it is as though we are like a sales force responsible for the advertisement and successful marketing of God the product. Beavering away with tracts and sermons, using fair means and foul to achieve a conversion, we have done our bit if we persuade the punters to try the commodity. Much evangelism takes such an approach: it seems to me that this is a concept of God as a product of religion, unable to speak for himself, incapable of forming relationships without our assistance, unable to respond except when the button with the correct name is pushed; not really a living God at all.

That is not how I now see God. God is free, untamed, and does not need or wait upon our programmes and structures. Mission is not ours, it is God's, and the determining feature of the mission of God is unconditional love: all that heals and nurtures, all that is just and speaks truth, all that is brave and good and a source of grace. If we love God and want to nurture our spiritual being, it will help us to let go of our traditional church agendas, and simply track God, like we might track a wild deer, or a badger in the woods. Look for the signs of God's presence and grace and life in people: and humbly reach out for the privilege of becoming a companion of that journey, that road to Emmaus, the journey on foot of the human soul in the company of the Christ; as a learner, as a friend.

When I approach the bedside of a person who is dying, and the loved ones who may also be there, it is with no thought of altering their spiritual agenda to the shape of my own priorities. Sometimes I feel shy to intrude, or apprehensive and doubtful of being able to help, especially if someone has told me this person has much pain and fear and needs a skilled companion. Sometimes I feel an instinctive flash of joy, that this encounter of the spirit will be something very special. But I always know that Christ is already there, that aware or unawares, the being of this dying man or woman will have met, touched, danced with, the living God.

There is no need at all for me to explain doctrine or nudge anyone towards religious belief. If God is with us, really here, then the actual presence of God is the thing that matters, not God's labels, or a striving for a monopoly on grace.

Sometimes as we get to know one another better, the person I am with will ask me about my faith, my insights and beliefs; maybe ask me what will happen to our souls when we die, or what God expects of us. And then I say only the truth: what my insights are, whether I know a thing, or only think or guess or hope that thing. But deep inside myself, I trust God. I believe in a God who lives and is with us, a God who is good and whose love is unconditional. My being rests in the company of that God, like everybody. The friendship of the holy does not have to be paid for by doctrinal aquiescence. In fact, religious doctrine can sometimes obscure our vision of a God who is good. All we need to do on the Emmaus road that we journey together is to walk and chat, listen and continue. The insights will come; they cannot be forced, nor do they need to be.

Then, there is the question of heaven and hell, salvation and damnation, who's in and who's out. Not a big issue for some people, a concern they shrug and dismiss, being focused on life here. But for others it is a terrifying matter. For those gripped

81

by the anxiety that permeates this area of religious belief, there are a variety of possible responses.

Some may violently reject all religion, hate it helplessly while the wound of fear it made is still not healed inside.

Some become very rigid adherents of religious organizations, employing strict codes of belief, dress, behaviour and ethics to ensure they do not lose their personal salvation or betray the demands of their jealous God. These people can be difficult spiritual companions, as loud and unequivocal condemnation of people whose outlook differs from theirs is sometimes seen as part of their religious duty, and friendship with people of a different spirituality is seen as dangerous.

Others again struggle with clinging shame, especially if they have transgressed against religious codes of sexual ethics, by divorce, or having many sexual relationships, or finding their sexual orientation to be the wrong one for their religion.

The more I consider the traditional teaching on heaven and hell, the more nonsensical it seems to me. The basic outline is that God will allow people into heaven, or send them into hell, according to whether they believed and acted upon the doctrines of the Church. This is complex at the outset: does one have to believe and act on all of it? What about Jesus' command to love and forgive? If one forgave ninety-nine out of a hundred people, would one go to heaven for the ninety-nine or to hell for the failure (ah, it would be the latter; I know this guilt trip!).

Then, if we managed to confine and suppress and distort our humanity to fit the spiritual requirements, and clung to our place in heaven, shut the door on the tormented screams of the damned thrown into hell by our God of 'love' – would it not be hell itself to be saddled with the presence of that jealous and vengeful God forever?

Sometimes I have pondered on the personnel of heaven and hell. I have known Christians who were very clear in their expectancy of who would be in which destination. It seemed to be a mixed bag in both camps – but on the whole I found my friends to be among the ones going to hell.

There are some theologians who refuse to discuss heaven and hell at all, seeing the discussion as theologically naive: there are others who say that there is heaven or hell, but those are states of being, not situations. Hell is the state of being cut off from God, outside God's joy and bliss and love (and note that even those theologians who say hell is not a place still use language like 'outside' and 'cut off'). Heaven is the correspondingly contrasted experience of the presence of God. The cruelty of this view is that it likes to retain a little of God's gift for the damned: emotional sentience, so they can feel miserable and lonely; spiritual sensitivity, so they can feel their emptiness and lostness. No. The one who can feel pain is not lost to God. The lost and the empty and the forlorn are cradled in the healing hands of God, and no exclusive and self-righteous theological attempts to create a spiritual inner ring will dictate to God or limit the love of God, or curtail God's gentle, redeeming mercy, this side of the grave or beyond.

Then what do we mean by salvation? What I mean by it is the liberation of the human spirit from all that cows and fetters and shames it, by the graceful presence of God, to free, unafraid, generous, abundant life. That, and the finding of peace: peace being not only the equilibrium of the soul, but the energy to act and work for the extension of God's justice and love, peace that comes from the confidence of knowing oneself loved, comes from the trust in the hands of the Creator to be strong and safe, not hands that will crush the life out of me, or drop me, or throw me away. The purposeful peace of Jesus, whose spirit rested in God, not for withdrawal from, but for engagement with, real life and real people.

There is a thing people say: 'Get a life! Get real!' I think they have an insight into salvation.

## DIGNITY, HUMILITY AND RESPECT

The time in which a person draws near to death, the times when a person is bereaved, are times of great spiritual power. These are times when faith can be rocked to its roots, or found for the first time. To accompany people who are dying or bereaved on that part of their life journey is to be given a great trust, a great privilege. These are times when the soul shines very clear; they are among our moments of sharpest reality.

In such times a person is also very vulnerable. Pain, nausea, weakness, incontinence, mental confusion, helplessness, loss of privacy and independence – all these may be part of terminal illness. And both for the person dying and their loved ones, there is emotional turmoil; anger, tears, fear and uncertainty.

Good spiritual care approaches people in these spiritually charged times with humility and respect, not making assumptions or imposing other agendas, taking time to listen, giving enough space for fear and grief to be allowed into the open, for the new identity of the changing self to be explored.

Good spiritual care is also gentle with the vulnerability and fragility of people who are dying and bereaved. It is attention to the spiritual quality of care, as well as good nursing and provision of necessary equipment and facilities, that will allow the time of death to be met with dignity.

All of us hope to die with dignity. The possibility for that lies partly in our own hands; for dignity will be an attribute of our own soul. But partly the dignity of our death will be the gift of others. Needing each other is integral to human spirituality: it is in relationship that we make our destiny. It is by working together that dignity in dying is achieved.

# 7

# AIDS, Fear and Love

AIDS is a hot subject in nursing, social services, education and theology today. In the present climate of emphasis on community-based care rather than institutional care, and given that many AIDS patients are younger people, with a network of potential carers about them, people who have AIDS may be more likely than most terminally ill people to be cared for in the community than in an institution. But, as I listened to people whose lives have been affected by AIDS, I became aware that the determinant of care in the community is attitude in the community. Journeying alongside people living with and dying of AIDS showed me above all else that love and fear are the opposite ends of the spectrum of attitudes in community care. With people who have AIDS, and their loved ones, good spiritual care must address the issue of fear:

> fear of contagion;
> fear of sexuality;
> fear of dying;
> fear of the judgement of God;
> fear of physical weakness and of dementia;
> fear of rejection (and the shame of rejection in the past).

Some of these are fears common to all people facing death. AIDS is unusual in that it generates all the usual fears and some of its own as well. There is another fear that attaches to the situation of people dying young, which is often the case for people who have AIDS, whereas other illnesses less commonly strike predominantly younger people. This is the fear that (in contrast with older people dying) as their friends and family are mostly still alive, so their concept of death does not carry the hope of being reunited with loved ones lost, but rather a fear of being sent ahead into loneliness. This is a fear of being cut off from friends and family, a miserable vision of the holidays, eating, sex, parties, family life, sunbathing, shopping, friendships and fun of this life all going on without me. Me going out into the strange, bodiless, unknown silence of death, to face God alone and be forgotten by everyone I loved here.

Such concepts of dying operate on a subconscious level, and so remain unarticulated, and are the more powerful for that. For this reason, it may be especially important for people with AIDS to be very clearly reassured that they are loved, both by human friends and by God. They may need to receive reassurance that they will never be forgotten, that the relationships they are part of here will have contributed to their friends' lives and personalities indelibly; the love they gave, the gift of themselves, is part of life here for ever, and can never be lost.

Another fear expressed to me by a young gay man with HIV antibody positive status, was the fear that his parents would want to become his main carers when he became ill. His parents loved him, but were uncomfortable with his homosexuality. His relationship with them had been one of guarded and limited openness, determined by the extent to which he felt they needed to be protected from knowing details of his personal life. He was haunted by the fear of one day suffering from AIDS-related dementia, nursed by his parents in a physical and social environment at odds with all his own choices, no longer sufficiently in control of what he said and did to keep the secret of himself from them to the end. It was not their disapproval he feared, it was their pain.

Pastorally, AIDS offers very interesting possibilities for observing personal relationships. Because many of those who die of AIDS are young, they can offer spiritual carers many insights into the impact death can make on an intact relational network – family, friends, lovers. This is especially helpful, because it may help prepare spiritual carers to offer support to groups of friends and family bereaved by sudden death where the person dying is young – in a motorbike accident, for example. In such a scenario there may be no time to acquire the insights needed for support skills, and the time spent with people bereaved by AIDS may provide invaluable insights.

Many of those who die of AIDS take the trouble to educate themselves, to an unusually sophisticated level, about their illness and changing physical state. This gives carers the chance to see and learn from the psycho-spiritual process of coming to terms with death in people who understand their prognosis and the implications of the progression of their illness more than most.

Many of those who die of AIDS are homosexual men and, because homosexual partnerships have traditionally been culturally beyond the pale for our society, this offers an opportunity to find out about sexual partnerships less stereotyped by tradition than most heterosexual partnerships, more creatively diverse, rich in insights and surprises.

The presence of AIDS sends out its ripples beyond the dying person and his/her loved ones: nurses and social workers and volunteers are also disturbed by its presence; reminded of their own mortality by the concept of infection; confronted with their own sexuality and cultural assumptions, challenged to be more 'out' about their own perspectives and relationships.

As I began to research and think around the whole subject of AIDS and the quality of care for people with AIDS in the area where I live, my research took me alongside a dying man and those who cherished and cared for him. Research receded and love began. He became not an object of study but a special friend. His friends became my friends. Months later, reworking the notes I made, for this chapter of my book, I realize that some of my favourite friends are the legacy of his illness and dying. It was true what we told him; he will never be forgotten – he changed the whole fabric of our lives, what we are. He left us a gift of loving.

And all ministers who want to become the companions of people on their life's last journey must understand, theology is not a cut-and-dried matter of the intellect: the being of God knows passion and tears; theology is learning to love, and without love, Christian theology is no more than the spilling of empty words.

I have left the notes I made in the present tense, as I wrote them; they are the record of that very special companionship on the journey.

There is a story told of St Francis, from the early days before his spiritual character and vocation was formed. The story tells that he was riding over the plain that lies beneath the city of Assisi when he saw a leper coming towards him on foot.

Francis had a horror and loathing of disease, especially the dread leprosy, and panic and disgust filled him as he and the leper moved towards each other. Then he struggled inside with the recollection that he was supposed to be trying to follow Jesus – Jesus who loved and healed and touched the lepers, who treated them just the same as everyone else, as people to be loved. Feeling ashamed of himself, and without giving himself time for his resolve to fail, he put his horror aside, got down from his horse, and ran to meet the leper. They stood then on the plain, two men on foot, on equal ground; and the leper stretched out his hand to beg alms. Francis gave him some money, but first he kissed the hand that begged for small change, and he hugged the sick man in his arms.

Francis turned away, and remounted his horse, trembling a bit probably: scared, joyful, relieved. Once on horseback, he looked all round that open plain, and the plain was spread before him unbroken; there was no leper anywhere to be seen. Francis had embraced his own fear. To stand one's ground before the thing one dreads, offering there not loathing but love, is to encounter angels.

And here's another story about angels. Today John lies dying. His four-year fight since HIV progressed to AIDS is nearly over. Today his chest is filling up, his breathing is erratic and his body, skin and bone, is running out of energy.

Last night his partner and his buddy recounted a story to me. For some time now, John has suffered from increasing dementia, which scares, embarrasses and upsets him. But the dementia has revealed the enchanting, witty, whimsical thinking of his subconscious mind.

'Who is the man who puts things on your back?' he had asked.

His partner and his buddy were puzzled. Things on your back? His buddy, a medical herbalist, wondered if he meant some kind of liniment. Or a cloth, or something? What? They tried out these suggestions on him.

'No,' said John, '*wings*.'

'Oh!' said his partner, '*wings*. Who is the man who puts

wings on your back? Well . . . I guess that would be . . . God?'
'Mm.' John was satisfied with this suggestion.

AIDS is the modern equivalent of leprosy, not that leprosy
has vanished from the earth, but that it has ceased to be
used as a myth for our time. Today AIDS is the myth of
our society, the disease we identify as that which tells us
the story of our morality, our betrayals, our death. AIDS,
a spectre more awesome than cancer, has become for our
generation 'the terror that stalks by night', in that its presence activates an almost hysterical fear of contagion, a fear
in which irrationality is betrayed by the lack of correlation
between the magnitude of the fear and the likelihood of
infection.

I respected and admired one of the nurses I talked with for
her honesty in describing her own struggles to come to terms
with the concept of AIDS. As part of her training she was offered the chance to visit the London Lighthouse. Once there,
she found herself left alone on a seat while her companion
went in search of a cup of coffee. A man came up to chat to
her, someone who worked at the Lighthouse. She explained
that she was a visiting nurse, learning about AIDS treatment.

'I have AIDS,' he told her. He talked to her about his
illness, and she was impressed by his candour. After a while,
he shook her hand and he went on his way.

'I couldn't get to the basin fast enough to wash my hands
after he'd gone,' she admitted. Even though she is a nurse.
Even though she knew there was no danger of transmission
through ordinary social contact.

And this nurse went on to say how she had struggled with
her own prejudices about homosexuality. Later I learned
from someone else that it had been the discovery that a
dearly loved colleague is gay that had helped her come to
terms with the concept of different sexual orientation.

'But I don't know what I'd do if I saw them kissing,'
she said.

Step by step that woman is learning to overcome her ir-
rational fears and prejudices, by meeting real people, loving
real people, who are gay, who have AIDS. Real people.
Fear is more catching than AIDS is, but for fear there is an

antidote. As the first epistle of St John says, 'There is no room for fear in love. Love drives out fear.'

If I put my hands to my face, I can smell the man whose hand I have held, whose arm I have stroked, whose head I have kissed, whose clothes and bed I have helped to change this morning. I feel no need to wash away the memory. The bedside of someone that close to the face of God is a place of angels.

AIDS is also equivalent to leprosy in terms of social myth in that, because it activates fear, it resonates in the sphere of the religious, it has acquired a mythology, it has extended its territory to the regions of symbol and imagination.

The regions of myth and imagination are dominated by language, because language is the precursor of abstract thought.

Thus it is that, in asking a man for his impressions before and after visiting a hospice for the first time, I heard the by now familiar answer that he had been amazed to find it a place of life and laughter and flowers. Asked what he had expected, he replied: 'I thought it would be a bit grim . . . and quiet.' People do. Knowing that it is, among others things, a place where people come to die, they project upon it unawares the vocabulary of death that conditions their expectations: 'The Grim Reaper. As silent as the grave. Scared to death.'

Thus also the myth of AIDS has become attached to other myths of fear in unconscious levels of the mind. Fear of the alien is one such fear myth, because our characteristic response to otherness is fear.

An example of this is the teenage lad I listened to in the HIV testing clinic. This was his second appointment, and at the first he had explained that he had presented for testing because he had become very frightened that he might have picked up HIV from a girl with whom he had had unprotected sex ten months ago. Asked what it was that made him so anxious, he said it was because the girl was foreign – French, as it happened. It later transpired that, a month after that, he had also had unprotected sex with an English girl: but he hadn't even thought to mention that, because she wasn't foreign, so had not carried the threat of the outside, the other, that the French girl had.

Fear of the other also manifests powerfully in the responses of heterosexuals towards homosexuals. John's mother, weeping, described how hard it is to protect the secret of her son's illness, not telling neighbours and acquaintances, only trusted family and friends. She spoke of the stigma attached to the illness, because of its association with sexuality, and how that added to the suffering of watching her son dying. She told me how John had broken the news to family members, and confessed afterwards that he had expected them to want no more to do with him, and what relief he had felt on realizing they were still there for him. And it was not until HIV progressed to AIDS that John had told even his doctor of his positive HIV status – and that he told through the clinic nurse. He couldn't break the news face to face.

John's partner Simon spoke of an encounter with a medical professional. Simon, in discussing John's illness, had begun to cry. 'She held out a Kleenex to me and looked away. It was like she was saying, "Oh, no, the poof's going to cry."'

For many, gay men especially, the presence of AIDS has caused a contemplation of their own mortality, and this has in turn awakened buried fears. I spoke with one man, who has campaigned for and cared for people with AIDS, and he told me of his own fears. He described his upbringing as a devout Roman Catholic, and affirmed that his faith was still living and important to him. He told me how, in discussing the death and funeral of a friend, he had mentioned in passing how he himself would like a Requiem Mass said when he died. Then, pondering the conversation later, he had become uneasy. As a gay man with a partner he knew his Church considered him to be in sin, that he should not take Communion if he wanted to play by the rules. It had therefore been some while since he had been to Mass. When he died, would they say a Requiem Mass for him? And if they wouldn't, did that mean, maybe, God would have no welcome for him? What *would* happen to him when he died? He confessed this fear with tears in his eyes, fear not only of rejection here, but rejection in eternity.

The Church, which likes to think of itself as an agent of forgiveness, needs to be forgiven much. In its cruel dogmas and heartless rigidity, it has threatened too much of damnation, rejection, abandonment, crushed the already wounded, spoken out of turn, in its stridency drowned the whisper of God who loves.

Fear of contagion, especially where there are sexual connections, especially when the understanding of those connections is muddled, also imparts a quality of shame – the 'stigma' John's mother spoke of. I was intrigued, observing a group of school students playing an educational game designed to illustrate the transmission of a virus, to hear them saying 'Ugh, you're dirty, you've got it, you're dirty!', and displaying in their body language a mimicry of vigorous withdrawal and rejection, while taunting the 'infected' one loudly.

As the teacher of the class said, 'At this age, their own attitudes are not really formed. What they bring to the classroom are their parents' attitudes.'

A serious, even dangerous consequence of fear is that people who are afraid, and who do not confront, maybe do not even identify, their fear, unwittingly permit their actions to be determined by their fear and not by reality, because their fear distorts their perspectives on reality.

An example of this is the difficulty experienced by a nurse in one nursing home who is responsible for educating her colleagues in the hygiene precautions necessary in care procedures, to guard against the spread of HIV infection.

Some care staff find it difficult to regard nursing home residents as sexual beings, and cannot embrace the concept that *anyone* they are nursing may be HIV positive, whether or not they are 'AIDS patients'. Carelessness in the disposal of wet and soiled bedlinen and clothes, and of incontinence pads, and failure to understand that blood and other body fluids are potentially dangerous, show that staff have not grasped the facts of the situation. Interestingly, in an effort to comply with more appropriate nursing procedures, a notice was posted asking staff to ensure that faecally soiled (but not wet) linen should be bagged separately for the laundry. This simple association of faeces–dirt–disease–nastiness with its dangerous inaccuracies and insufficient grasp on reality is a product of the fatal bonding of fear and ignorance which limits the possibilities of real education.

AIDS, like all tragedies, is coloured with theatrical glamour. With characteristic creativity, gay men have turned the tables on the stigma of what was in the early days perceived as a gay epidemic. Buddying, red ribbons, beautiful memorial quilts, World AIDS Day, high-profile media coverage, widespread educational projects, theatrical productions, national and local helplines, time and talent volunteered, money outpoured: no other illness has found such a response to the challenge it offered as the response of gay men to AIDS.

The London Lighthouse, aptly named, represents a triumph of positive attitudes. It is extraordinary and delightful that a centre for the care of people with this most dreaded sickness should have become a social magnet, a place to go, to meet people. The London Lighthouse represents a triumph of hope, of love over fear.

Particularly interesting also is the Terence Higgins Trust, which has waged war on both the ignorance and misery surrounding the disease. In the early days of the epidemic, when Terence Higgins died of AIDS in a London hospital, his partner Rupert, not being a family member, was not allowed to visit him there. His desperate attempts to gain access to Terence's bedside finally succeeded, and he came bringing a gift of ice cream, to find the curtains drawn around the bed. He was asked to wait elsewhere, unaware that staff were trying to resuscitate Terence. The attempt was unsuccessful, and Terence died before his partner had a chance to see him. Thank God, things are better than that now. Today, the Terence Higgins Trust's buddying scheme offers a radical and exciting model of community care, a viable alternative to familial networks of support. The Trust also offers by far the most eye-catching and professionally presented educational material about AIDS available.

St Paul writes that our battle is not against flesh and blood, but against the powers and principalities that rule our age, and AIDS has become one of the battlegrounds for that struggle. It has thrown into sharp relief that life-threatening illness can be an opportunity as much as a disaster, that fear can call forth courage and love as much as condemnation and abandonment.

George Herbert, writing in the seventeenth century, described the presence of God, with its transformative power, by using the image of the alchemists' stone; the stone whose extraordinary powers enabled it to turn base metal into gold. He spoke in these terms of God's grace:

> This is the famous stone
> That turneth all to gold;
> For that which God doth touch and own
> Cannot for less be told.

Grace is there, where the base metal of fear, dull and obdurate, is turned into the gold, riches incomparable, of love. I have heard preachers call AIDS the judgement of God on sexual behaviour. I have seen AIDS be the tough and painful context in which the miracle and mystery of grace emerge. 'That which God doth touch and own' – the bodies wasted by AIDS; it is a good thing that God so often chooses to ignore the judgements of preachers, and walks instead along the unexpected paths of love.

John's partner, although their relationship was not an easy one, its future uncertain, chose to stay with John until he dies, trained as a Registered General Nurse in order to be prepared to care for him as necessary, and has travelled with him through the many crises of his illness.

John's bedside is a circle of friends, of laughter and love. Last night his partner told of a phone call he had received from John the previous night.

John announced with conviction that he was phoning about the party to be held the following night (there was no party planned, this was John's dementia). He said he wanted to know about the cats.

'What about the cats?' his partner responded, bewildered.

'Well, can they come? Have they got anything else on?' came John's rather tetchy reply.

'Er . . . no,' responded his partner. 'No, I think they're free.'

Why do I tell that story? I tell it because the way to break the bonds of ignorance and prejudice is for people to meet people, for the stranger to become a friend, for the dreaded bearer of disease to become the endearing, quirky bundle of individuality that makes up a real person.

The challenge of AIDS for our time is not physical, it is spiritual. Everyone has to die of something, and no one can become invulnerable to disease or untimely death. But everyone has a choice whether to let fear or love dominate their lives, whether to confront the adversary in the form of prejudices that warp the being on the inside or in the form of helpless, suffering human beings who embody that fear on the outside.

The day I met John he was lying prone in his bed, unresponsive, his eyes nearly shut. Two friends sat quietly at his bedside. I introduced myself, and John remained unresponsive to my presence. I had a sense that maybe John was not quite as out of it as he looked, and perhaps needed time to assess whether or not he wanted to know me: so I stayed and chatted on with his friends a while. Eventually a volunteer came round enquiring if we wanted a cup of tea or coffee. John's friends and I declined politely, at which point John's eyes snapped open and he said, 'I'll have some tea. And a doughnut. Please.' With delight, I realized that I was looking into the eyes of a very naughty child indeed! And those light blue eyes then scrutinized me very carefully – I have come to learn that they are the eyes of a very shrewd and perspicacious man. They still burn bright in a face that is so, so emaciated now. And when they light up in a smile, more rarely now the going is getting grim, I know that I will miss him when he dies. Maybe tomorrow, maybe the next day. I will miss him very much.

John died of AIDS
at seven o'clock
last night.
He died peacefully.

# Deciding to Die

Sooner or later, in accompanying people on their last journey on earth, one has to confront and consider the complex moral issues of euthanasia and suicide.

This subject, more than any other, is one which leaves me sitting at the word-processor keyboard, gazing at nothing, lost in thought, unable to begin. Sometimes it seems that the more that is said about euthanasia and suicide, the further from reality one travels. I have listened to many people on this subject, and I think I have learned a lot about those people, but not much about euthanasia and suicide. My instinct was to leave it alone but the book seemed incomplete without a chapter on this. My expectation is that the words I have to add will tell you more about me than about deciding to die.

Death, life's other face, is *essentially* mysterious. It offers questions, not answers. Living wisely is about learning patience with one's own uncertainties and contradictions, and being compassionate with other people's. Life and death cannot be plumbed for moral certainties: there are none, and there is a reason for that.

Jesus said, 'I am the way, the truth and the life,' thus offering us an understanding of ethics, ideology and human being that arises not from conformity of the self to facts and concepts, but is instead relational – one that arises co-dependently from love. If Jesus could say, 'I am the truth', that gives us an insight into his silence in answer to Pilate's question, 'What is truth?' Maybe his silence was not a refusal, but a response. 'What is truth?' asks the man, and the Christ just stands there before him, offering the truth below and beyond discussion and ideas; truth that offers itself as a 'me', not as an 'it'.

If we understand that truth is better understood as a person than as a fact, a doctrine or a concept, it may help us to see why it is so elusive, so hard to verify, so self-contradictory; and so beautiful as well.

Issues of life and death defy moral pronouncements because they belong to the realm of truth that is personal.

'Fact – it is wrong to take life' is a meaningless statement, as soon as one starts to think about it. In a world of abattoirs, international debt, shared exhaust fumes, the unexamined decision to destroy our own life and the life of others is a constant factor for all of us. The milk on our cereal at the breakfast table was in nature intended for the four-day-old calf that was slaughtered as the useless by-product of the dairy industry, unless it was reared as veal for the dinner table. Or, if our ethical pondering does not extend as far as other species, the beef in our spaghetti bolognaise came from cattle fed on the cereal that would have saved the life of human children in poorer parts of the world than ours.

Life and death cannot be separated. The medicines that save our children's lives are tested on countless animals dying in vivisection laboratories. The wealth of our country that ensures our health and comfort was made on the backs of the colonies. The car I drive to be at the bedside of someone who is dying is puffing out the clouds of smoke that are killing the living – the whole planet.

Fixing on euthanasia and suicide as one aspect of the interface between life and death salves consciences but is shallow thinking. Life and death cannot be separated or resisted: that is, indeed, the heart of the Christian gospel.

I do not believe it is natural or good for a person to seek euthanasia or suicide; but I do believe that it is sometimes right. It is not natural or good, in the sense that *wanting* to die arises not out of a positive experience of death (which is unknown and therefore awesome and alarming for all of us), but out of a negative experience of life. Euthanasia and suicide are indicators of personal agony, signs that things have gone badly wrong. They are sought not because of a misguided sense of moral rectitude, but because, for the one who seeks them, life has become unbearable, intolerable, so that whatever terrors death offers, it has to be preferable to this life, now.

For a person suffering from serious physical, emotional or mental illness, there can be a profound gap between experience and belief. A belief that God is good and provides for our needs, provides grace sufficient for our circumstances; but an experience that one's resources are insufficient for this circumstance, that the only grace needed here is a way out. Or a belief that life is a gift, a beautiful, wondrous gift; but an experience of being helpless to partake of it, of not having the talent to use it, unwrap it, take it: a gift best left for others.

Nobody really wants to die. If there were someone who could change things, salve the wound, whatever it is, make it better, then life would be chosen for its sweetness and delight. But sometimes death enters into life, invades life, makes life a living hell, a living death: and the need to escape becomes acute.

Perhaps the most important thing is that, whatever our own views, if we are companions on someone else's journey, we should remember whose journey it is, and not try to drag them along our own path.

## EUTHANASIA

At present euthanasia is illegal in the UK. Whatever the pressure of circumstance or horrific symptoms, any person with the power of life and death over another would do well to remember that in this country euthanasia is against the law, both in the sense of the letter of the law and in the sense of the deeply felt ethical consensus of the population. However one might view that, however one might reflect that if those who make laws nursed people this particular one would change, and swiftly; none the less, the present reality is that euthanasia is illegal, and if a case of euthanasia comes to court, the outcome may be very serious indeed.

'Living wills', in which a person may record the desire to be allowed to die rather than be repeatedly resuscitated or kept alive by artificial means, may be helpful and may be respected.

The difficulty here is weighing up so much of the unknown. Most people would probably prefer to die from a stroke than be extensively disabled by a stroke: but it is not so easy to tell which stroke will kill you and which disable you, or how much of the disability will be permanent and how much temporary: therefore it is not easy to tell which act of intervention will prevent merciful death in an otherwise fatal stroke, and which will improve the quality of life in a serious, disabling, but not fatal stroke.

Life and death are mysterious by their very nature; they will not be prised open. We can never know what would have happened; we can only do our best with what is. And part of what is, is sharing the world with others whose ethical stances are quite different from our own.

It is helpful to consider the difference between passive euthanasia and palliative care. Both recognize that a person is dying. Passive euthanasia recognizes that death is inevitable, and withholds life-preserving treatment (such as antibiotics to prevent infection, or maybe food and water) in order to allow death to come more swiftly. Palliative care, such as is offered in a hospice, also recognizes that death is coming, but rather than seeking to hasten it, seeks simply to maximize the quality of the life that remains, regardless of whether that shortens or lengthens it.

When somebody is dying, talk often turns to the taking of life, many terminally ill people expressing a wish not to be a burden on others or to be put out of their suffering. This should always be taken seriously, but at the same time the carer should beware of interpreting what is said in a manner favourable to the carer's ethical outlook rather than the dying person's.

Sometimes an expressed wish to die so as not to be a burden on others is an indication that worrying problems, such as the provision of adequate nursing care at home, or the resolution of financial or other practical difficulties, need attention. A private and independent person may feel unable to ask for help, and feel an abhorrence of imposing on family or friends, especially for intimate physical nursing or assistance with personal financial concerns. To such a person, in terminal illness, death may well seem the only solution, whereas, in fact, learning to relate with others may be one of the avoided, necessary and richly rewarding tasks, very much a part of life itself, a transformative and beautiful part of living before the time comes to die.

Other times, the expressed wish to die just looks like common sense to everybody. Moralists are not always aware of the circumstances in which some people end their lives. If you are one of those whose body has to be taped together in order to be laid out after you die, one of those whose body systems have failed to the extent that the soles of your feet have dropped off or your face has been mostly cut away by surgery then invaded and overtaken by an advancing tumour – then death may reasonably be considered welcome, and grand talk of the moral value of life lived to the bitter end, leaving the moment of death, as well as the manner of dying, to God's goodness, may ring hollow.

### SUICIDE

There may be many reasons to choose suicide. For someone bereaved of a deeply beloved friend, the longing to follow them may be overwhelming, and the world may be empty without their presence.

Someone else may be drawn to suicide by a deep sense of personal inadequacy, insignificance and worthlessness, sometimes an inexplicable sense of shame. Strangely, this often happens with people who are very beautiful, gifted and accomplished.

There are others who long to slip away from the party, to walk out into the sea, or jump from a high building, without really knowing why.

Then there are those who are afraid: facing financial collapse or the disclosure of a dreadful secret; those who are bullied – prisoners, schoolchildren, people of a minority sexual orientation in an inflexible social environment. Sometimes there is fear of the future; fear of the progression of a terminal illness, perhaps, and the process of dying.

And there are those who are in anguish, mental or physical – anything ranging from loneliness to the agony of physical disintegration – who simply seek an end.

Is it enough to clump them together morally, and say suicide is wrong? And would this sort of categorizing ever help us to understand?

Most pain is eased by friendship, if only a little. Those who find a companion on the journey may also find the journey worthwhile.

There is a great gulf between suicide and euthanasia in terms of the impact they make on those they bereave. Euthanasia is often perceived as a gift, a service:

'We couldn't let him suffer any more.'
'We had to help her, do something.'

Suicide, on the other hand, is a very scarring form of bereavement. The ones left behind may feel guilty, feel that they should have been able to heal, to help. Sometimes the bereaved cannot allow themselves to mourn, because they feel culpable of the death.

For those who are companions on the journey, here are some principles offered as starting-points in considering how best to respond when euthanasia or suicide are mentioned:

- To assist suicide or perform an act of euthanasia is against UK law.

- Each one of us has his/her own path to walk, personal tasks to face and decisions to make. It is not for us to impose our moral or ethical framework on someone else, nor is it helpful to attempt to take responsibility for someone else's existential dilemmas and decisions.

- To listen with complete, focused attention, hearing others' stories, entering their world, taking them seriously, treating them with deepest courtesy and respect, is not only a precious gift in this circumstance, it is also a rare one.

- To assist others in deep spiritual turmoil, especially when that is compounded with, or manifested as, physical pain, it is vital that our own peaceful presence remains strong and centred. According to our own spiritual or religious affiliation, we should practise a discipline of prayer and meditation, so that we remain a source of healing radiance.

  In connection with this, we should also focus on the one we are accompanying in our prayer or meditation, for their peace, wholeness of being, and fidelity to their real perception of truth.

- A circumstance viewed externally is often quite different from how it is experienced internally. Sometimes, the process of death may be appalling to look upon, appearing gruelling and cruel, yet be experienced as peaceful and graceful for the dying one. In the same way, people who look as though they have everything going for them may be transfixed in agony of soul for which they can find no remedy. While no one should underestimate the suffering caused by helplessness and pain, it is nevertheless true that the time leading up to death can be a period of powerful spiritual enrichment, a journey precious and blessed for both the dying one and the bereaved, despite its grim and harrowing struggles.

## MY OWN VIEW

Euthanasia and suicide arouse strong positive or negative reactions, often rooted in powerful memories and life experiences, and it is important always to recognize and respect that, treading sensitively and retaining balanced judgement, bearing in mind one's own bias as well as that of others.

I myself have always been a person with strong suicidal inclinations. I am very fearful, especially of disapproval, and very easily discouraged. I have at times in my life very seriously contemplated suicide, at the worst times being prevented only by two things; my knowledge of how damaging and destructive bereavement by suicide *always* is to friends and family members, and by fear of offending God.

At this moment in my life, I do not feel drawn to suicide, but I expect I will again, as that is the tendency of my personality.

My own suicidal tendencies, and my strong Christian beliefs, caused me to ponder at length on this issue, and the conclusion I have come to at the moment, which I offer you tentatively, is as follows.

The source and ground and centre of all being is God (or Reality, or the Light of Being, or Love, or Truth – whatever name you are comfortable with). The being of God radiates to the physical dimension; matter is the 'heavy' end of the matter–spirit spectrum. Matter – our bodies, the earth, the living world – is holy. But matter is the peripheral edge of the sacred: as the Holy One creates and renews and outpours Holy Spirit, it starts with spirit and radiates outward to matter. The centre of all that is, is spiritual.

When we die, a door opens for us, and we go into the heart of Holiness, of Spirit, of Light. We are welcomed into the presence of Love's Self. This life, this teeming, vibrant earth, with all its glory and all its tragedy, is like a veil, a diaphanous wrap, upon the being of God. It seems so real and solid to us, but it is all shadows and illusion seen in the light of the inner Holiness that lies at the heart of being.

Here, we are exiled; this life is to prepare us, to make us wise and beautiful in readiness to enter the presence of the Beloved at death.

All of us are travelling nearer, all the time. Some of us know it, and some are oblivious, but our journey into the centre never falters for a moment.

We are like travellers standing on an escalator as it moves upwards. One by one, those who are ahead of us reach the top, and step on to solid ground, and all the while our turn approaches.

Or we are like those bidden to a wedding: the organist, the celebrant, the bridesmaids, the groom, the bride, the ushers, the guests. One by one, the timing according to our tasks, we set out from our houses, all heading for the same place, each in our time.

In the same way, our lives are directed towards death. From a very young age, our physical body begins to decay, to withdraw, to loosen its hold on our spirit. We see others go through the door of death, and we know our time will come too. The demands and vicissitudes of life come like the waves of the sea, offering us endless opportunities to learn wisdom, humour, strength of spirit, gracefulness, courage and love, all in preparation for our entry into the presence of God.

To say we are all directed towards death is not morbid or negative, only true. Death is not a horrible thing, it is a beautiful thing:

> ... we are already the children of God
> but what we are to be in the future has not yet been revealed;
> all we know is, that when it is revealed
> we shall be like him
> because we shall see him as he really is.

> (1 John 3.2, JB)

When we die, we are invited in from our long exile; home, into the presence of the Living God. *Invited*. It is not for us to violate that holy presence, to intrude there before we are called. It is not for us to force the door or climb over the fence: we have to wait until the way opens.

This is not to say that those who will not wait, whose need for mercy and peace becomes so urgent, so desperate that they force the door, are unforgiven, rejected or condemned. It is not in the nature of the Beloved to receive them like that. God is all mercy.

But to force the door in some way breaks the web, hurts the pattern.

Now I say this knowing that it is glib and shallow in the face of the hideous life circumstances that some people face. And I have no doubt that there are circumstances in which I would hesitate no more than a moment to end either someone else's life or my own (a child dying hopelessly of terrible wounds after an explosion in a battle, for example). And to do so might not be a failure of trust in God's love, but an ultimate act of trust that he will forgive even this.

Neither life nor death is our enemy; it is all gift. The best way to meet it, to live it, is by living in the present moment, engaging with what is reality *now*. Imagined futures are the source of much distress.

As a final thought on this subject, it is also worth noticing and pondering, as we journey alongside others towards death, that death does seem in some strange way to be something we *do*, as much as something that happens to us.

Nurses often remark that a patient is 'clinging to life', or 'will not let go'. It is a common enough thing to see someone wait for the arrival of a loved one, or a longed for event, before they die; and some people choose a rare moment of solitude, quiet, private souls, who want to die alone. Some people need permission to die, need to be reassured that dependants will be cared for, or a particular unfinished task carried out; and then they can die in peace.

John's Gospel records Jesus as saying: 'I lay down my life in order to take it up again. No one takes it from me, but I lay it down of my own accord. I have power to lay it down, and I have power to take it up again . . .' (John 10.17–18). Bearing this in mind, it is not so easy to make a moral distinction between death entered actively or passively. The martyr's death, the soldier's death, we weight with glory. It is not simple. Nor should we expect it to be, because it is a measure of its sacredness that we tread cautiously here.

Whatever our choices, though, we should not delude ourselves that to die is to make an end. Those of us who have been privileged to spend time with people who are dying sometimes catch glimpses of moments when the veil flutters, and we see beyond. Rays of the peace and beauty occasionally filter through. The doorway into death, whatever else it may be, is not the way out. It is the way in.